Total College Success

What You Absolutely Need to Know BEFORE Starting College

Gary A. Harris, Ed.S.

Academic Architects
Lenoir City, Tennessee

Copyright © 2019 by Gary A Harris

All rights reserved. This book contains material that is protected under the Federal and International Copyright Laws and Treaties. Any unauthorized reproduction, reprint, transmission in any form, scanning, photocopying, recording, information storage and retrieval, or use, in whole or part, of this material is strictly prohibited without the prior written permission of the copyright holder.

Academic Architects
www.AcademicArchitects.com

Systems Solutions Innovation Design Group, LLC
www.SSIDGroup.com

Publisher's Note: The author and publisher have made every effort to verify and ensure that the information in this book was correct at press time, and makes no representation, warranties or guarantees (expressed or implied) in regards to the accuracy, fitness, applicability, or completeness of the subject matter contained in this book. The author and publisher do not assume and hereby disclaim any responsibility or liability to any party for any loss or damages of any kind, or disruption, caused by interpretations of the subject matter, or errors or omissions, whether such errors or omissions result from negligence, accident, or any other cause. This book is for informational and entertainment purposes only. The views and opinions expressed in this book are those of the author alone and should not be taken as expert advice.

Published 11/1/2019

Total College Success / Gary A. Harris, Ed.S. -- 1st ed.
ISBN 978-1-7333956-0-1

*This book is dedicated
to my two beautiful nieces
Kimberly and Melissa*

Thanks!

I want give my sincerest thanks
to the proofreaders of my book.

Clay Lundy

Anne Marie Orr, MA

Table of Contents

Preface xi
Why I Wrote This Book xi
Approach of the Book xiv
Conventions Used in this Book xv

Section 1 - About College 1

Chapter 1 - Introduction 3
Main Benefits of a College Education 3
Alternatives 4
Very Important Suggestion 5

Chapter 2 - Terms and Credits 7
College Terms 7
College Credits 9

Chapter 3 - About College Courses 11
Types of Courses 11
General Education Courses 12
Core Courses 12
Electives 13
Course Focus 14
Course Levels 16

Transfer Courses 17
College Credit through Testing 19
Grade Point Average (GPA) 21
Withdrawals and Incompletes 24
Transcripts 25

Chapter 4 - About College Degrees **27**
College Majors and Minors 27
Types and Levels of Degrees 28
The Associate Degree 29
The Bachelor Degree 30
The Masters Degree 31
The Specialist Degree 32
The Doctorate Degree 33
Doctorate Degree Tip 35
Additional Degree Types 36
Certificate and Diploma Programs 37

Chapter 5 - About Colleges and Universities **41**
Public Colleges and Universities 41
Private Colleges and Universities 42
Ivy League Universities 43
Government Study 44
Sub-Categories of Colleges and Universities 45
Political Bias 46

Chapter 6 - Accreditation 47
Regional Accreditation..48
National Accreditation...50
Specialized (Programmatic) Accreditation....................................51
Other Accreditation 52
Caution about Accreditation...53
Other Acceptability Considerations..53
Degree Mills..55

Chapter 7 - About Online Education 57
Types of On-Line Learning Activities...61
Two Specialized Teaching Approaches 63

Chapter 8 - Cost 65
Tuition 65
In-State Tuition versus Out-of-State Tuition................................66
Special In-State Tuition Programs for Non-Residents 67
Additional Fees..69
Large State Universities 70
As Seen on TV 71
A Financial Comparison of Public and Private Institutions 71
Financing Your Education..76

Chapter 9 - School and Course Quality.......................................79

Chapter 10 - Final Thoughts about College............................ 85

Section 2 - Selecting a College and Degree Major.................. 89

Chapter 11 - Picking Your Degree Major.............................. 93
Some Real-World Stories 93
Government Study 97
Four Ideas 100
Final Thoughts 108

Chapter 12 - Selecting Your School and Getting In............. 109
College Admissions 109
Research the Schools 112
Research the Programs... 116
Research the Instructors... 117
Aggressive Admissions Tactics 119
Entrance Exams 123
Red Flags 125
Final Thoughts 127

Section 3 - In College and Beyond 129

Chapter 13 – Planning Your Degree 131
Degree Plan.. 131
Sequencing Your Courses.. 136

Course Load 139

Chapter 14 – In College 145
Tips for Writing Projects and Papers... 145
Plagiarism.. 148
Internet Research and Computer Literacy 150
Netiquette, Email, and Respect... 152
Additional Suggestions... 153

Chapter 15 – After College 157
Continuing Education... 157
Professional Development Courses 158
Continuing Education Courses 158
Professional Certifications.. 158
Professional Associations... 159
Books and Periodicals 160
Consider Another Degree 160
The Bottom Line 161

Chapter 16 - Conclusion 163

About the Author.. 165

Preface

Why I Wrote This Book

At 17 years old I joined the Air Force and became a Munitions Specialist, also known as an "Ammo Troop". I enjoyed the military and eventually retired. While I was in the military I spent a lot of time thinking about what I would do after the military, especially being a Munitions Specialist. There are not many jobs out there that require the skill set to build up and maintain bombs, missiles, rockets, and mines. I did pick up some good skills though, such as operating a forklift, warehousing, supervision, and management. These are all good jobs, but it is not what I wanted to do for the rest of my life, and jobs in management usually require a college education. So I decided to go to college early in my military career.

It took me a while to get my first degree. At that time, the Internet was not around and being transferred to other military bases often required me to switch schools, which added additional time to completing my education. Additionally, at first I really didn't know what area I wanted to get my degree in. I started studying law enforcement, but then decided not to go in that direction. I switched to studying electronics, but then that didn't turn me on either. So then I started taking general education courses (math, science, English, etc.) and management courses. I eventually completed an associate degree in Work Center Management. A friend of mine had a home computer and it piqued my interest in computers and later I earned a bachelor's degree in Management Information Systems (a combination business and information technology degree). Afterwards, I knew I wanted to continue my education but there were limited graduate programs where I was stationed at the time. I took a few graduate courses, but didn't go further due to being stationed at a new base. I eventually found a degree program that interested me and that would further my career. I earned a masters degree in Engineering Management. It complimented my bachelor's degree in many ways. In addition, I do have a personal goal of earning a PhD. I was accepted into three different PhD programs, but dropped them due to my dissatisfaction with the programs and the instructors. I talk about this a little bit in the book. I wanted to move on so I decided to get an "intermediate" advanced graduate degree, an Education Specialist degree. I was accepted into two Education Specialist Degree programs. I dropped the first program due to dissatisfaction in the program and later completed an Education Specialist Degree in Instructional Technology at another school. At that time I still planned on pursuing my PhD but thought I would get a second master's degree first. The reason for this is that the credits for the second master's degree will reduce the number of credits I will need for the PhD thus saving me money, plus I may be able to use the master's degree to get some additional work while I am working on my PhD.

I started getting a strong interest in the field of higher education early in my career. I taught for the Red Cross for over 11 years and have over 10 years experience teaching at the college and university level. My interest in education changed to distance and on-line education due to the advent of the Internet and my background in computers. I picked up a certification in distance education and landed a job with a large nationwide on-line university as a contractor developing on-line courses in Information Technology. I developed several courses myself and managed the development of over 100 on-line courses for the school and was hired on as the Dean of Business and Information Technology. Unfortunately, due to reorganization they closed that division of the school and moved it to Wisconsin, which didn't interest me because I was living in Florida at the time. I later managed the development of several on-line professional development courses and certificate programs for a professional association. As of the writing of this book I am currently teaching on-line courses for two state universities. I also started a business that provides course and curriculum development to colleges and universities.

I have a lot of time invested in the research of various education programs, to include reviewing more than 500 colleges, universities, and other school programs in many subject areas. I have surveyed many college administrative staff and faculty regarding their programs and have read many books and papers on the subject. On many occasions, I have been approached by family and friends for suggestions and advice regarding approaches to education. I discovered that there is a lot of misinformation and misunderstanding about colleges and college programs. For many students they only have the information that the school provided them. And in many cases it is exaggerated or flat out wrong. For these and many other reasons, I wrote this book to pass on my research and experience to assist future and current students with their pursuit of a college education. I believe this book will be helpful and eye-opening.

Approach of the Book

The approach of this book is NOT to provide you with a step-by-step process or checklist for selecting a degree program or a college or university. The approach of this book is to provide you the information you need to make a sound judgment on selecting and pursuing a degree program or a college or university yourself. I have read many books and articles that attempt to provide "step-by-step" instructions, or "how to" instructions on selecting your major, picking a college, or financing your education. Where these books fail is that they give you a cookie-cutter, "one size fits all" approach to these subjects. The truth is "everybody is different", every situation is different, and every college and university is different. One size or one approach does not fit all. This book's approach is to educate you about the various aspects of choosing a college major, choosing a school, financing your education, and planning your education so you will be able to effectively research schools yourself, ask the right questions that fit your situation, develop your own thoughts, and help "you" to make a sound judgment. This book is not there to try to hold your hand every step of the way. You have graduated high school. You are an adult now. The hand-holding is over.

Conventions Used in this Book

Compared to other books, you should notice something a bit different about the way I write. I write in a conversational style as if I were speaking to you in person face to face. I do not write as if I was writing a thesis, doctoral dissertation, or a user's manual. I take a common-sense approach to things and provide "real-world" examples. I'm a firm believer in simplicity and brevity. I make every attempt to get to the point and cover the material in detail without rambling. And, I will tell you things in this book that you will not find in other books. I hope that you will like this writing style and that this book will be helpful in your endeavors.

I use the terms "college", "university", and "school" synonymously in this book. In addition, I don't name any specific schools or people, or provide any lists of schools or programs. There are many books on the market where you can obtain these lists. But, why should you? You can find those lists on the Internet for free. You can get the information you need from the horse's mouth by visiting the websites of the schools you are interested in. You can easily find various college review sites and read postings from students that have attended those schools and have even reviewed specific professors. And a good amount of that information will probably be more current and un-biased than what you will find in a book. In addition, I have provided links to most colleges and universities on my professional website, www.GaryHarris.com. Just go to the menu item "Useful Lists" and you will find the links. You can use those links to get you started.

It is very important to know that no two schools are exactly the same. They all offer different degrees, different levels of degrees, and often have different interpretations of programs. For example, if you take a course in business at one school, and then go to another school that offers a course with the same course name, chances are it will be different. One school may offer degrees up to the bachelor level while another school may offer graduate degrees. For these reasons, you will see me use the words "usually", "typically", and "normally" extensively throughout this book when describing different aspects of a school or college program. It is important to keep in mind that a feature or aspect at one school may not be applicable at other schools.

This book focuses on colleges and universities in the United States. Colleges and universities in other countries often take different approaches and have very different naming conventions and types of programs.

Section 1
About College

Important Note: If you have not read the preface to this book, please go back and read it first. It has some very important information that will help you understand parts of this book. It is a quick read.

This book starts with providing some basic and general information about college. It is very important to have a solid foundation and understanding about the basic aspects of college prior to starting your journey. If you don't understand the symbols on a map, how can you ever get where you want to go? That is the purpose of this section.

As I mentioned in the preface I use the terms "college", "university", and "school" synonymously in this book. However, there is a difference between a college and a university. A college is a school that usually offers programs at the undergraduate level. These programs include certificate and diploma programs through the 4-year bachelor degree level. A college is usually made up of one or more schools, such as a "School of Business" and "School of Liberal Arts". A university is often made up of one or more colleges and schools. It can offer anything that a college offers in addition to graduate degree programs.

With that in mind, every college and university is different - and - there are exceptions to the rules. For example, there are some colleges that offer graduate degree programs and there are some universities that don't offer doctorate level degrees. This is important to keep in mind when researching schools.

Although I will not be using any specific school names, I will probably make a lot of schools mad at me in this section of the book. That is ok, because I am going to say it like it is. You will get information that a lot of people won't tell you, especially the schools themselves, starting with accreditation. There is a lot of misleading information out there about accreditation. You will be getting the straight story in this book. One point that will be covered in detail that you absolutely need to know is cost, which is probably one of the most important factors about selecting a school. So let's get started.

Chapter 1
Introduction

I want to start this book by pointing out two important benefits of a college education that you should keep in mind as you read through this book. These benefits are usually the reason why people go to college.

Main Benefits of a College Education

There are several benefits to getting a college education and you are probably aware of most of them. However, I want to briefly highlight the two main benefits, 1) increased opportunities and 2) increased earning potential. Both of these benefits are directly related to each other and "usually" if you have one, you will have the other. The important thing to know about these benefits is that there are different levels of these benefits. In other words, you could have a higher level of increased opportunities and earning potential with one type of college degree versus another. This is usually depends on the area and level of your degree, but often experience. I will be providing some information and ideas to think about that can help increase your opportunities and earning potential by making some sound decisions in choosing your direction in college.

Alternatives

This book makes the assumption that you have decided to go to college. However, I do want to point out that there are a lot of good jobs and careers that do not require a college education. For example, a good welder that knows the trade well can lead to a rewarding career – and the world needs welders. My brother Glen was a welder. It turned out to be a great career for him. He worked on small projects as well as huge projects, such as building military ships at a shipyard in California. He learned the trade so well that he was able to do things that other welders could not do.

Another good career that does not require a college education is Truck Driver. And until they figure out how to "beam" cargo from one location to another like in Star Trek, we will need truck drivers. The pay is good and you get to travel.

There are many good and rewarding careers that do not need a college education. You can go a great distance with many of these careers, such as starting your own business. Take the two examples above, Welder and Truck Driver; if you are good, you can start your own business with both of these professions. You have to be really good though. You should start thinking early in your life what you want to do and what you want out of your life. If you are in high school, start thinking now. But keep in mind that you are never too young or too old to start.

I cannot end this section without mentioning that the military, law enforcement, fire fighting, and some medical fields are also good careers that usually do not require a college education. These are needed specialties, have good job security, and are very honorable careers.

As I previously stated, this book makes the assumption that you have decided to go to college. This book is not a large book because it does not need to be. It is a small read, but packs a lot of information. You will get a lot of ideas and information to think about when selecting your route (area of study) and degree program. When it comes to finding and selecting your college, I will provide some important insights about schools that you won't hear from other people or read in a book.

Very Important Suggestion

This will probably be the most important piece of advice I will offer in this book. If you are currently in high school, don't quit. If you have dropped out of high school, go back. If you are an adult and don't have a high school diploma, there are adult high schools that you can attend. These days, you can get a high school diploma on-line. But whatever you do, get your high school diploma. Even if you are not planning on attending college, get your high school diploma. If you don't get your high school diploma, you're opportunities will be limited. What do you think that a potential employer might think of when he/she reads on an employment application that you are not a high school graduate? If you are competing for a job, chances are that most, if not all, the other people competing for the same job will have a high school diploma. Who do you think will get the job? If you do want to go to college, most colleges require you to have a high school diploma. The bottom line - finish high school! I cannot emphasize this enough.

Let me tell you about my high school situation. I did drop out of high school at age 17 to join the Air Force. I did get a GED diploma to join. But after Basic Training and Technical School, I got smart and went to an Adult High School at my first military assignment and received my regular High School Diploma. I am grateful that I did. Since then, I retired from the Air Force, started three businesses, and finished an Associate Degree, Bachelor's Degree, Master's Degree, an Education Specialists Degree, and currently working on a PhD. I attribute much of that to finishing and earning my high school diploma. I do wish I would have finished high school prior to joining the military. But I have made up for it.

Chapter 2
Terms and Credits

There are two basic aspects about college that is important to understand before getting deeper into this book - college terms and college credits. Without having a solid understanding of these elements, other parts of the book may not make sense. You might have already been exposed these aspects, but there are different traits that you need to be aware of. You may come upon a school that implements terms and credits in a way that you are not familiar with.

College Terms

Schools often divide their academic year schedules into "academic terms", often just called "terms". There are two systems that are typically used, the semester term system and the quarter term system.

The semester term system originally had two six-month terms (fall and spring) splitting a year in half. In most schools that use this system the two terms have morphed into three terms a year (fall, spring, and summer). The fall semester typically runs 16 weeks from August to December. The spring semester usually runs 16 weeks from January to May. The summer semester is usually shorter and runs eight weeks from June to July.

In the quarter term system, there are usually four terms a year, which often follow the seasons. The four terms are about two and a half to three months long and usually run from September to November, December to February, March to May, and June to August. These terms are shorter than semester terms.

Now comes the fun part. There are three unusual aspects about these term systems. First, an academic year does not usually run from January to December. Depending on the school, an academic year usually starts around August or September and ends in June or July. That is why you often see a school year listed as a two-year notation, such as "school year 2017-2018". The second unusual aspect is that you will see a wide variety of adaptations of the term system they use. This is usually identified by the start date of the individual terms. And third, many schools often have two sub-terms in a single term. You usually see this in a semester term system in the spring and fall terms because they are longer. This means that you can take more courses in a single term. But be careful. These sub-terms are half the size but are required to contain the same amount of work to meet credit hour requirements. Please keep this in mind when reading the section on course loads later in the book. The bottom line is that every school is different so it is very important that you understand the system used at the school you select.

College Credits

A "college credit", often referred to as a "credit hour", is simply a system to measure your effort in college. It is usually based on the number of contact hours per week, and the number and length of terms in a year. It allows for a school to offer smaller courses for fewer credit hours or larger courses for more credit hours. I am not going to get technical on how they are calculated. That is not important. What you need to know is that there are basically two different types of college credit hours: Semester Hours and Quarter Hours. As you probably have figured out, the system they use is based on their academic terms they have adopted, which we previously discussed.

As previously mentioned, schools that use semester hours usually have two or three "semester" terms a year. Usually, a typical year of courses consists of 30 semester hour credits. Also, typically a standard course is usually 3 semester hours. Thus a standard full year would consist of 10 courses, depending on the school.

Schools that use the quarter hour system usually have four quarter terms a year. Quarter terms, which are about 10 to 12 weeks long, are smaller than semester terms so courses have to be compressed. They usually have a very different weighted numbering system than semester terms. Usually, a typical year of courses consists of 45 quarter hours (versus 30 semester hours in a semester system). A typical course would be 4 to 5 quarter hours long. Thus a full year would consist of 9 to 12 courses, again, depending on the school.

There are calculations available to convert the credit hours from one system to another if you are transferring to a school that has a different numbering system. The important point here is to understand the number of credits earned by a single course and how many courses you may need to take in a year.

Important Note: Please note that I will be using the Semester Hour system for my examples in this book.

Chapter 3
About College Courses

In this chapter you will gain an understanding of the different types of courses that colleges and universities offer that make up degree programs. It is extremely important to have a solid understanding of the different types of courses because it will help you in selecting your degree program. You will be able to compare one program to another in terms of the types of courses offered and how much effort is earmarked toward the major subject area of the program. For example, if one program only required you to complete 30 credits in your major and another program requires 60 credits in your major, you will graduate with a stronger understanding of your major subject by selecting the second program requiring more credits. Remember from chapter 2 that credits measure your level of effort in a course. Let's jump into the types of courses.

Types of Courses

There are basically three main types of courses in a degree program. It is important that you have an understanding of these types of courses when selecting a degree and making your selections and planning out your degree program. The three main types of courses in a degree program are general education courses, core courses, and electives. There are some schools that have some different names for these, but they still will fall under one of these general categories.

General Education Courses

In your first four years of a college degree program, most schools require a specific amount of general education courses. They are usually determined by the type of degree, state laws, and accreditation requirements. These subjects will be covered later on in this book. General education courses are usually liberal arts and science courses that include subjects such as English, mathematics, humanities, social sciences, and natural sciences. Most schools usually have a required set of courses but will usually allow you to select some courses to meet the general education requirements. For example, most schools require two specific courses in English composition. However, they will usually allow you to select from a list of social or natural science courses, but will usually require a specific amount.

Core Courses

Core courses are the courses in a specific subject that are required in a degree program. They are usually in the subject area of the major and/or minor of the degree. For example, if you are in a business degree program, you may be required to take specific courses in economics, accounting, marketing, human resources, etc. It is important to understand what the required core courses are for a degree program, and what subject matter they cover. The reason being is that you may enroll in a degree program and find out later that it is really not what you were looking for. Let me give you a "real-world" example.

After my son finished his AA degree he transferred to a state university to get his degree in Information Technology (IT). During his first term at the school he realized that the courses in the degree program focused a lot on information technology "theory" and not what he was interested in, which was programming. After researching IT degrees at other state universities, he found one that met his needs and transferred to that school where he eventually graduated from. So the point here is to not just rely on the degree program names and course names. Read and understand the degree program description and the course descriptions.

Electives

Electives are courses in a degree program where you get to select the courses. There are basically two types of electives, program electives and open electives. Program electives are courses in which you must select a certain amount of courses or credits from a specific list of courses in your program, often in the same area as your degree major. For example, if you are in a business degree program, you may be required to select a certain amount of business courses (program electives) that are above and beyond the required "core" courses for your degree program. Open electives are courses that you can take on any subject. Often, there may be a level requirement for the courses, which I discuss later in the chapter. I always suggest selecting courses that will benefit your degree program when selecting your open electives. In other words - don't select underwater basket weaving as an open elective because it will not benefit your degree program such as in business or information technology.

Course Focus

Courses can "broadly" be focused in two different directions: 1) theory and research, and 2) knowledge and application. Courses that are focused on theory and research are based on the study and research of ideas, conceptions, and propositions of principles or methods. These types of courses foster creation and innovation, such as inventing a new material or technology. Courses that are focused on knowledge and application are based on the study of known facts and acquiring and applying new skills. In these courses you gain knowledge and learn how to do something, such as programming a computer or managing a business.

Often the degree program you are in will dictate the focus of your courses. For example, if the degree you are seeking is in marketing, you will be taking courses focused on learning marketing and applying the skills in a business environment. Sometimes these two focus areas cross paths. For example, engineering subjects are often involved in both theory and research and knowledge and application. These are important concepts to keep in mind when selecting a degree program because not everyone is a good fit for careers in theory and research, or knowledge and application subjects.

In addition, as you earn higher level degrees, such as, masters and doctorate degrees, you often move from one focus to another. For example, the courses in an undergraduate degree in business will focus on knowledge and application of business subjects. When you move into the graduate degree programs, the focus may change to theory and research, especially at the doctorate level. At the doctorate level most graduates usually work in research, development, and education.

Course Levels

Similar to high school, during the first four years of college there is a designation that identifies where you are in school. You are considered a "freshman" during your first year, sophomore during your second year, junior during your third year, and senior during your last year. There is one important thing that you need to be aware of in regards to courses. As you progress through the years in college, the course levels progress as well. They become more advanced level courses. A course in your third or fourth year of school is much more advanced as the courses in your first two years.

Courses in most schools usually are assigned a course number. The course number usually designates the level of the course and the year in college that you would normally take that course. For example, the first course in English composition may be numbered ENGL-100, where "ENGL" designates it is in the area of English language courses and "100" designating it as a first year or freshman level course. You would normally take this course in your first year. A more advanced course in English composition may be numbered ENGL-200. This would indicate that the course would normally be taken in your second year and that it is more advanced than ENGL-100 as identified by the course being in the 200 series. In addition, you may be required to take ENGL-100 before you take ENGL-200. That is known as a prerequisite, which is discussed in detail later on. Courses in the 300 series would normally be taken in your third year and 400 series in your fourth year. The higher the series number, 400 versus 300, would indicate a more advanced course. Courses in the 100 and 200 series are often referred to as "lower level" or "lower division" courses, whereas courses in the 300 and 400 series are often referred to as "higher level" or "higher division" courses. Graduate level courses are usually numbered in the 500 series and higher, depending on the level and the school. It is important to keep in mind that all schools don't use the same numbering system. The example above is simply a common system used. When you are researching a school, you need to learn their numbering system so you can plan your education.

Transfer Courses

When you take courses at a college or university and then later switch to a new school, in most cases you will be able to transfer the credits for those courses you earned to the new school. However, most schools have rules pertaining to transferring in courses to their school from other schools. For example, they may limit the number of credits or types of courses you can transfer in. Those rules are often very different from one school to another. It is extremely important that you find out what those rules are when you are researching specific schools and you have taken courses at another school that you would like to transfer in. Below are some items you should find out about when researching schools.

1. It is important to determine if the courses you want to transfer in are directly related and count towards the core courses in the new program at the new school you are considering. If not, find out if they can be used as program or open electives.

2. If you want to transfer courses to a school that is regionally accredited, in most cases the courses you are transferring in must be from a school that is also regionally accredited. I cover accreditation in chapter 6 in detail.

3. Most schools have a limit on the number of credits you can transfer in. Find out what that limit is. It is usual that the higher the degree, the fewer number of credits will be allowed for transfer.

4. Most schools have a rule that limits the age of the courses that you want to transfer in. If it has been several years since you completed the courses you desire to transfer, you should find out what the course age limit rule is for the new school. I personally do not believe in this rule. I believe that if

you completed the course – you earned the credits – no matter when you took the course.

5. One of my biggest pet peeves is that most schools will not provide an "unofficial" evaluation of the courses you want to transfer in before you apply to the college. In most cases you will need to apply to the new school and request "official" transcripts to be sent to the school before you will be able to find out if the courses will transfer. This can take a lot of time and be costly if you are looking into several schools. So keep this in mind when you are doing your research. Also keep in mind that just because a course has the same name and even the same description as a course in the new school, that does not guarantee it will be accepted for transfer. I have personally seen many examples of this.

College Credit through Testing

There is a fantastic opportunity for you to reduce the number of courses you need to take for your degree, along with reducing the cost of college. That opportunity is college credit testing programs. The way it works is simple. If you have knowledge in a certain subject, you may be able to take a test, and if you pass it, you may be able to earn college credits for a specific course and don't have to take that course. I have personally completed almost a full year of courses (27 semester hours) through testing.

As of the writing of this book, the college credit testing programs include the College Level Examination Program (CLEP), AP (Advanced Placement) exams, DANTES DSST tests (for military only), and Uexcel examinations. You can easily find information for these programs on the Internet. I strongly suggest that you look into these as they can save you time and money towards your college education. Some schools have their own testing programs where you can challenge a course with a test. Additionally, if you have completed a professional certification, I have seen some colleges grant credit for certain certifications. These options would be worth asking about.

Preparing for the tests is fairly easy. There are many books on the market as well as short and cost effective courses on the internet to help you prepare for the tests. If you are a recent high school graduate, you may be prepared enough to take some of the tests already, such as English, math, or science. If you have taken higher level math classes such as calculus in High School, you may be able to knock out several math courses. It does not hurt to try these tests. If you don't pass a test, it does not affect your overall grade or your standing in school.

The credits don't get added to your transcript unless you pass the test and are accepted by the school. One important point though – in selecting a school, part of your research process should include finding out what and how many credits from college credit tests they accept. Not all colleges accept all the different types of tests and most have a limit on the number of test credits they will accept. Also, keep in mind that these are only available for undergraduate programs. And finally, if you are in the military, many of these tests are available to you at your Base Education Office either free of charge or at a greatly reduced price.

Grade Point Average (GPA)

Your GPA is simply the average of your grades. It is very important to have a good understanding of the GPA system at your school and to monitor your GPA during college. Most schools use the 4.0 scale where a point value is assigned to a specific grade. Table 3-1 is a simplified "high level" look at this scale:

Grade	Point Value	Grade	Point Value
A	4.0	C- / D+	1.5
A- / B+	3.5	D	1.0
B	3.0	D-	0.5
B- / C+	2.5	F	0
C	2.0		

Table 3-1

Keep in mind that not all schools use this scale and some even use a modified version of this scale. You will need to understand the scale of the school you select. To figure out your GPA, you simply add up the (point values times the number of credits for each course you have completed) and then divide by the total number of credits. For example, assume that you completed the following courses in Table 3-2:

Course	Grade	Credits	Points (Grade X Credits)
ENGL-100	A (4.0)	3	12
ENGL-101	B+ (3.5)	3	10.5
HIST-100	B (3.0)	3	9
BUS-100	A (4.0)	2	8
TOTALS:		**11**	**39.5**

Table 3-2

Chapter 3 - About College Courses

Calculation from Table 3-2:
Your GPA = 39.5 / 11 Credits = 3.59 GPA

For undergraduate degrees a passing grade is usually a C (2.0) or better. For graduate degrees the passing grade is usually a B (3.0) or better. Some doctorate programs require even higher GPA's, such as a 3.2 or 3.5 to earn your degree. If you take a course and get a grade lower than a "C", I would suggest retaking the course to bring up your GPA. Check with your school on their rules. With some schools, retaking the course may keep the first course from affecting your GPA. Some schools have a grade forgiveness program that will wipe out the first grade from your transcript. So it is important to know what your school offers.

Now - you are probably wondering why I am talking about GPAs and grades. I bring this up to make an important point. You should try to get the best grades in college as you can. If you are still in high school, this applies to you as well. Don't just be satisfied with a passing grade of a C in your college programs (or in high school). There are three main reasons for this. First, when you start looking for work, today - many companies often ask for copies of your college transcripts. If you are competing for a position and your GPA is a 2.0, and another individual has a 3.0, who do you think will have a better chance of getting selected for the position? The second reason is that if you ever might decide to get into a graduate degree program, your GPA is often one of the deciding factors for acceptance into a program. For example, most schools require at least a 3.0 GPA in your undergraduate work to get into a master's degree program. In addition, many schools require a 3.25 to 3.5 GPA in your master's degree to get into a doctorate program. The third main reason for doing well in college is that your GPA is often a main factor for obtaining scholarships and grants to finance your education. Remember, college is not cheap. For these reasons, I strongly suggest that you do the best you can once you are in school. And if you are reading this book and still in high school, I recommend you do your best in high school as well for the same reasons. Colleges and universities will be looking at your high school GPA for acceptance and scholarship reasons. There is no reason to settle for "just" a passing grade.

Withdrawals and Incompletes

When you drop a course after starting it, it is considered a "withdrawal". Withdrawals usually <u>do</u> show up on your college transcript, often as a grade of "W". They usually do not affect your GPA; however, having several of them in your transcript does not look good. If you have several withdrawals, it could affect a future employment opportunity or entrance into graduate

Chapter 3 - About College Courses

school. So be careful of overusing them. There are justifiable situations in which you may want or need to withdraw, such as medical reasons, but again, try to keep them to a minimum. Additionally, most schools usually have a cut-off date as to when you can withdraw from a course to receive a "W" grade and to receive all or part of the tuition you paid for the course. You should find out the cutoff dates for each term you register for courses.

If you are unable to finish a course by the end of a term due to extenuating circumstances, such as for medical reasons, some schools and professors may allow you to take a grade of "Incomplete", or "I". In most cases you will need to complete the remaining work and turn it in by a certain date after the term is over. Additionally, if it is not completed and turned in by that time limit, often the grade would covert to a "Fail", or "F". So be careful with "Incomplete" grades. They can have a negative effect on your GPA. Every school has different rules about granting "Incomplete" grades - so make sure you know them up front.

Transcripts

Transcripts are simply a record of your college education. They contain a list of every course you have completed, or attempted, such as in the case of a withdrawal. They usually list the course name and number, the grade received, and your GPA. There are basically two types of transcripts, official and unofficial. An official transcript is sealed and sent from one school to another, or to an official source, such as an HR department. When transferring to a new school, or applying for graduate school, the school you are transferring or applying to will require official transcripts from all the schools that you have attended. They will only use official transcripts to accept transfer credits. An unofficial transcript is simply a transcript issued for the purpose of information only. You can and should request an unofficial transcript for yourself so you can have it for your personal records. Employers will often accept unofficial transcripts. When requesting transcripts from your school, there is often a cost for the transcript. Transcripts are usually requested through the registrar's office and official transcripts usually cost a little more than unofficial transcripts.

Chapter 4
About College Degrees

Usually the ultimate goal of attending college is to earn a college degree. Because of this - it is important to know what really a college degree is and what it takes to earn one. You may think that all you need to do is take a bunch of courses and you will earn a degree. In some cases that is correct. For some degrees it is not correct. In addition, there are different types and levels of college degrees and knowing their differences will help you select the best one to meet your career needs.

College Majors and Minors

A major is the main area or subject of study or specialization of a college degree. In a degree program, the majority of the courses taken for your degree "should" be in that area of specialization. Some schools allow for the ability earn a dual major degree. These programs often require additional courses with fewer electives.

A minor is similar to a major in that it is a set of courses that make up a "secondary" specialization in a degree program, usually requiring fewer courses than a major. Minors are often optional. If you go for a minor, I suggest that it be related to your major. For example, if you earn a degree in business administration, you may want to pick up a related minor, such as accounting or marketing. This gives you additional flexibility and increases you're your value to organizations and your opportunities. A degree in business administration with a minor in music appreciation does not. I agree - my minor in Psychology did not enhance my degree major in Management Information Systems. But I was not as knowledgeable then about degree programs. I would have chosen something different these days. However, my minor did help me understand people better, thus improving my business and personal relationships.

Types and Levels of Degrees

It is important to point out that all colleges and universities don't offer every type of degree at every level. When researching schools, it is important to determine the types and levels of degrees they offer and if they fit into your career path.

Levels of degrees basically refer to the rank or sequenced tier of a degree. It shows the level of your education. The higher the degree, the more advanced it is. The levels are usually expressed in the name of the degree. The levels, from low to high, include associate, bachelor, master, specialist, and doctorate. Associate and bachelor degrees are referred to as undergraduate degrees. Degrees above the bachelor level are referred to as graduate level degrees because you have "graduated" from a bachelor's degree program. Let's take a closer look at these degrees.

The Associate Degree

The associate degree is the lowest level college degree. It is usually earned after completing your first two years of college and is often referred to as a two-year degree. The three typical types of associate degrees are the Associate in Arts (AA) degree, Associate in Science (AS) degree, and the Associate in Applied Science (AAS) degree. The difference between the three different degrees is usually the amount of general education courses required and the major area of study. The AA degree is usually a degree in liberal arts and normally does not have a major. It usually completes all of your general education course requirements for the first two years of an undergraduate degree program. AS and AAS degrees usually require less general education courses and usually have a major. This gives you the opportunity to take more courses in your area of study. The AAS usually requires the least amount of general education courses. An example of a specialization for an AS or AAS might be an "Associate in Science in Business Administration" or "Associate in Applied Science in Computer Networks". Using the semester hour system, a typical associate degree would require 60 semester hours of credits (two years at 30 credits per year).

The Bachelor Degree

The bachelor degree is the next level up. It is usually earned after completing four years of college and often referred to as a four-year degree. The two typical types of bachelor degrees are the Bachelor of Arts (BA) degree and the Bachelor of Science (BS) degree. Both BA and BS degrees usually have a major. Like the AA degree, the BA usually requires more general education courses and the major is often in a liberal arts subject. Examples include "Bachelor of Arts in Psychology" and "Bachelor of Science in Computer Science". A typical bachelor's degree would require 120 semester hours of credit to graduate. You may think that is a lot of work. But an easy way to look at it is that it is only 40 courses – 10 courses (30 credits) a year for four years.

You do not need to have an associate degree to get into a bachelor's degree program. You would just finish those first two years of college as part of the bachelor's degree program. Many people simply start at year one and go through to a bachelor degree without ever earning an associate degree. In my opinion, this does not make sense. Why not earn your associate degree first? That gives you a credential half way through your four-year program that you may be able to use to get a good or better full time or part-time job while attending college. Also, what happens if you have a need to drop out of school or postpone your education for a while after the two-year mark? At least you would have an associate degree in hand. This could happen if there is a medical emergency in the family or your school funding runs low for a while.

The Masters Degree

The master's degree is the next level and the first of what is considered a graduate degree. When you get into the area of graduate degrees, there are a lot less "typical" items from one school to another. They vary greatly. For example, I have seen masters degree programs that require as little as 30 semester hours to complete the degree, and as high as 60 semester hours to complete the degree, and everything in between. It is usually around 30 to 36 semester hours.

Like bachelor degrees, the two main types of master degrees are the Master of Arts (MA) degree and the Master of Science (MS) degree. Both MA and MS degrees usually have a major. Examples include "Master of Arts in Sociology" and "Master of Science in Mechanical Engineering". Unlike the undergraduate degrees, graduate degrees only require courses dealing with the major and possibly a specialization. General education courses are no longer in the picture at this and higher levels, unless they are a prerequisite for a specific graduate level course, or you are earning master's degree in a liberal arts field.

The one typical aspect about a master's degree is that you must have a bachelor's degree to get into the program. There are often other requirements as well, such as an entrance exam or a specific GPA in your undergraduate degree. I will discuss this later.

The Specialist Degree

The specialist degree is an advanced graduate degree that is higher than the master's degree but below the doctorate level. It is mostly found in the areas of education and psychology. It usually requires around 30 semester hours (1 year of study) beyond the master's degree or in some cases 60 semester hours (2 years of study) beyond the bachelor's degree. The courses are usually at the higher graduate or doctorate levels.

In most cases, you are required to have a master's degree to be accepted into a specialist degree program. The specialist degree usually has a major, such as education, and a concentration, such as educational technology. For example, I completed an Education Specialist (Ed.S.) degree with a concentration in Instructional Technology with a focus on Learning Systems Design and Development.

The Doctorate Degree

The doctorate degree is the highest level graduate degree that can be earned. It is often referred to as a "terminal" degree because you are at the highest end of the education levels. When it comes to doctorate degrees, the requirements vary greatly from one school to another. A master's degree is usually required to get into the program. However, in some cases you can get into a doctorate program with a bachelor's degree. You would need to take more courses though. In my opinion, similar to what I previously mentioned about earning an associate degree before earning a bachelor's degree, I would recommend earning a masters degree prior to pursuing your doctorate degree. Again, this gives you a credential between your bachelor's degree and your doctorate that you may be able to use to get a good or better job while working on your doctorate. And again, if you have the need to drop out of school or postpone your education for a while, you would at least have your master's degree in hand. The requirements range from 60 to 75 semester hours beyond the master's degree to 90 to 120 semester hours beyond the bachelor's degree.

The two most common types of doctorate degrees are the Doctor of Philosophy (Ph.D.) and the Doctor of Education (Ed.D.). Both are considered research degrees, but the Ed.D. Degree specifically focuses in the area of education. Both degrees usually have a major, for example, "Doctor of Philosophy in Computer Engineering" and the "Doctor of Education in Educational Leadership". Often, these degrees may have a concentration above and beyond the major, such as the Doctor of Philosophy in Business Administration with a specialization in Project Management. Some doctorate degrees are known as Professional Degrees. These usually include Medical Doctor (MD) "required for physicians" and Juris Doctor (JD) "required for attorneys", and a few others.

Most people that get doctorate degrees, excluding professional degrees, usually go into teaching or research. In most career paths having a doctorate degree is not necessary. A bachelor's or master's degree will take you a long way. If you do plan on teaching, especially at the college or university level, or go into research, I would recommend that a doctorate degree be included in your educational plans. You can teach college with a master's degree, but your opportunities are limited.

Doctorate Degree Tip

There may be a way for you to reduce the number of credits and considerably reduce your cost to get a doctorate degree. Keep in mind that this will not work for all doctorate degree programs. This should be included when researching schools for doctorate programs. If you haven't earned a master's degree yet, you may want to take this into consideration.

Many doctorate degree programs will allow you use or transfer in credits from a master's or education specialist degree program. This would reduce the number of credits you would need for your doctorate. Let me give you my real-life example.

I have decided to pursue my Ph.D. Degree in Computer Science and have selected the school. The degree program requires 60 credits. However, I can transfer in 30 credits from a master's degree program. This would mean that I would only need to take 30 credits to complete my Ph.D. This would save me a lot of money - approximately $1,500 per course for those courses I transfer in. I already have a master's degree but the courses are not applicable to the Ph.D. program plus they are too old to transfer. So I could knock out a second master's degree to get those courses to transfer in. It will still save me that money by taking the second master's degree rather than taking the courses in the Ph.D. program. Plus it will give me another credential in hand to use while working on my Ph.D. If I would have known this before I started my first master's degree, I could have selected an appropriate masters degree. This is something you should keep in mind when thinking about a master's degree program.

Additional Degree Types

In the previous sections of this chapter I provided some "typical" or "usual" types of degrees, such as the AA, AS, BA, BS, MS, MA, Ed.D., and Ph.D. These are often referred to as "Academic Degrees". In reality, there are many other different types of degrees. From associate to doctorate, many colleges and universities offer specialized types of degrees. The best way to describe this is to provide some examples.

Examples:

> Associate in Accounting
> Bachelor of Business Administration
> Master of Public Administration
> Doctor of Business Administration

Chapter 4 - About College Degrees

Basically, you can fill in the blanks of these types of degrees with just about anything and some school "may" offer it, except for maybe underwater basket weaving.

Associate in _____
Associate in Applied Science in _____
Bachelor of _____
Master of _____
Doctor of _____

These are often referred to as "Occupational Degrees". If you research the Internet for different types of college degrees, you will find that there are literally hundreds of different types of degrees offered by different schools. I simply wanted to show you what is typical and give you a taste of what is available. But keep in mind, every school is different, especially in what it offers.

Certificate and Diploma Programs

Many colleges, universities, and other schools offer certificate or diploma programs in addition to college degrees. Certificate programs are often used for professional development and continuing education after college. I will cover this in more detail in chapter 14. A diploma program is often geared to prepare you for a job or career that does not require a college degree. For example, you can find diploma programs in Medical Assisting, Medical Coding and Billing, Bookkeeping, and Computer Network Administration. Keep in mind, these are great careers but these positions usually have limited growth and advancement potential and are lower paid positions than those that require a college degree.

Certificate and Diploma programs can be broadly categorized as "for-credit" or "non-credit" programs. The difference between the two is that the for-credit programs are made up of college courses for which you earn college credits for each course. You do not earn college credits for the non-credit program courses. For-credit certificate programs are usually more expensive than non-credit programs and the credits you earn in these programs can usually be transferred to a degree program. Certificate programs are often referred to as a Professional Certificate. Diploma programs are often referred to as a Career Diploma. As a reminder, a certificate program is usually used for professional development and continuing education and does not prepare you for a job or career where a diploma program does. Both Certificate and Diploma programs usually have a specialization.

Chapter 4 - About College Degrees

There are basically two types of "for-credit" certificate programs: undergraduate certificate programs and graduate certificate programs. Undergraduate certificate programs are made up of undergraduate level courses and usually do not have prerequisites to be accepted into the program. Graduate certificate programs are made up of graduate level courses and usually require a bachelor's degree to be accepted into the program. When involved in a degree program, sometimes you can earn a certificate while earning your degree. This is a good thing as it will give you additional credentials, providing that it is specialized and not just a duplicate of your degree. In addition, if you earn a certificate before you earn your degree, it may have a positive impact on your current job situation or help you get a part-time job in the interim. For example, if you already have a job, it could be documented in your performance evaluation showing that you are advancing yourself, or maybe even get a slight raise. My point is, if you can earn a certificate while working on your degree, go for it. It cannot hurt. I earned a graduate certificate as an online educator while earning my Education Specialist degree.

Chapter 5
About Colleges and Universities

Colleges and universities fall into two broad categories, Public and Private. Private schools can be further divided into For-Profit and Non-Profit schools. The main differences between these categories are their governance and funding sources. There are sub-categories to these high-level categories that I will cover later.

Public Colleges and Universities

Public colleges and universities are schools that are governed and regulated by a government, usually a state government. These include state universities, state colleges, and community colleges. Public colleges and universities usually have a very good selection of programs in a wide variety of areas. Some large state universities have opportunities in research not found in other schools. In addition, they are often subsidized by state government funds, but some do receive donations and endowments. Thus tuition costs are usually fairly low and opportunities for financial aid are sometimes better compared to private and for-profit colleges. However, public institutions usually have a higher tuition rate for out-of-state residents versus in-state residents. For this reason, it is recommended to look at schools in your state. In some cases, some state colleges and universities offer in-state tuition rates to students taking on-line courses no matter what state you are located in. In chapter 8 I will provide some information on programs where you can get in-state tuition if you are not a resident of the state where the school is located.

Private Colleges and Universities

Unlike public colleges and universities, private colleges and universities are not governed or subsidized by a government. A private college or university can either be a for-profit business or a non-profit organization. A for-profit college or university is what it says it is; it is a for-profit business, obtaining its funding solely from tuition and other fees. Some for-profit schools are owned by large corporations that own several schools in their portfolio. There are some good for-profit schools out there. But the bottom line is that they are in business to make money. A non-profit school is not supposed to be in the business to make money. They are in the business to provide an education to their students and are "usually" less costly than a for-profit school. Often, non-profit schools get some of their funding from donations and endowments. Some private colleges and universities are affiliated with a church. Colleges that are affiliated with a church are usually non-profit.

Chapter 5 - About Colleges and Universities

Ivy League Universities

Ivy League universities are private universities. As of the writing of this book, there are eight Ivy League universities in the United States. Ivy League universities are usually the most expensive universities to attend. Tuition costs can easily exceed $100,000 a year at one of these schools. This is odd to me because each of these eight Ivy League universities receive anywhere from $2 billion to $30 billion in endowments each year! Yes, that's "billion" with a "B". But they are still extremely expensive. Actually, a lot of big universities, to include some large public universities, have endowments into the billions as well.

The term "Ivy League" actually comes from the athletic conference they belong to, but also the term has connotations of a high level of academic excellence. However, you can get the same benefits and level of education at other colleges and universities, as well as have a much better selection of degree programs and at a definitely much lower cost. In addition, having a degree from an Ivy League university <u>does not guarantee</u> automatic career success, high pay, pay raises, and promotions. It "may" get you in the door easier in some places, but it will always be your qualities, capabilities, and work ethics that will determine your success - not the piece of paper hanging on the wall. Personally, if it was important to a company that I was interested in working for as to where my degree came from, other than accreditation considerations, I would not want to work for that company. I can only think of one reason why anyone would want to go to an Ivy League school and that is for the prestige (ego). Something to think about - "prestige" does not pay the light bill, or put food on the table. Also, when you finish school you may have a $200,000 or a much higher student loan bill to hang on the wall with your diploma. You might have it paid off in 20 or 30 years.

Government Study

I reference a government study later in the book about how the selection of your college major has an affect on your job opportunities and earning potential. Although this was not a major point of the report, the findings of the report also show that the difference in job opportunities and earning potential based on the "type" of school (public or private) is minimal. They were about the same. This means that those graduates that went to expensive private or for-profit colleges did not do any better than those who went to public colleges. This is another reason to think about going to an expensive school.

Sub-Categories of Colleges and Universities

In addition to the broad categories of public and private schools covered earlier, there are several sub-categories that schools can be classified into. These sub-categories include community colleges, liberal arts colleges, technical schools and colleges, business colleges, vocational schools, military academies, medical schools, law schools, schools of arts, faith-based, single-gender (all male or all female), and tribal schools. As you can see, most of the sub-categories are based on the subject matter taught at the schools, such as business, technical, or medical. All of these sub-categories of schools still fall under one of the broad categories of public and private schools. That should be taken into consideration. Keep in mind that schools will often charge more for their programs because they consider themselves "specialized". Don't fall into this trap; you can get the same level of education and often at a better cost at a public institution.

Recently I have noticed a trend of changes going on with community colleges in some states. Some states are converting their community colleges to state colleges, and are now offering bachelor degrees. The state of Florida has done this with most of their community colleges. These new bachelor degree programs are limited, but they are very cost effective.

Political Bias

One of my biggest pet peeves is that many universities are politically one-sided, especially at the large popular public and private universities. Often, college professors and students get in trouble at these schools because they may not have the same political beliefs as the majority of the school, or the school itself. I see this in the news all the time. No matter which direction you lean, you are going to school to get an education, and not to be indoctrinated towards a specific political ideology. But unfortunately that is happening a lot in our colleges and universities these days.

Politics should not be practiced in college, even if you are studying political science. You are not there to learn one way of thinking. My suggestion is to research this carefully to see if political bias has been a problem at a school that you are considering. It may be something you want to avoid. If you do decide to attend a school with a specific bias, don't let that come between you and your education, or let it change your personal beliefs or morals. That is not the purpose of a college education.

Chapter 6
Accreditation

Accreditation is a type of recognition that a school receives after it has gone through a detailed and rigorous evaluation process to ensure the school meets certain established standards. If a college or university is not accredited, chances are, the degree that you will earn will not be worth much and will not give you the opportunities and earning potential an accredited school will. If a school says they are accredited, don't just accept their word without asking a lot more questions, such as finding out exactly who they are accredited by. Keep in mind that accreditation does not guarantee acceptance of a degree or transferability of credits. That is up to each individual institution and employer. However, it does provide a much better chance of acceptability, depending on the accreditation.

There are different types of accreditation and it is extremely important to know the different types and to find out what type of accreditation a school has and exactly who they are accredited by. The two basic types of accreditation are institutional and specialized. Institutional accreditation is further divided into two sub categories, regional and national accreditation. Specialized accreditation is sometimes referred to as programmatic accreditation. This chapter will focus on regional, national, and specialized accreditation.

An important aspect of accreditation is that the accreditation agency must be recognized by the Council for Higher Education Accreditation (CHEA). All regional accreditation agencies and most national and specialized accreditation agencies are recognized by CHEA. So it is important to not only find out which organization has accredited a school, but also ensure it is an accreditation agency that is recognized by CHEA. You can see a list of accreditation agencies that are recognized by CHEA on their website at www.CHEA.org. It is a strong possibility that a school that is not accredited by an accreditation agency recognized by CHEA is a diploma mill. I will cover this a little later.

Regional Accreditation

Regional accreditation is considered the highest benchmark for degree acceptability and credit transferability. In most cases, a school that has regional accreditation will not accept transfer credits from other schools that are not regionally accredited. This is often spelled out in school catalogs regarding their credit transfer policies. In addition, if you are planning on teaching in the future, especially at the college level, most of those faculty positions usually require you to hold a degree from a regionally accredited college or university. As I previously mentioned, all regional accreditation agencies are recognized by CHEA.

There are only six regional accreditation agencies. It is easy to determine if a school has regional accreditation or not. You can go out to the specific regional accreditation agency's website and see if the school you are interested in is listed. I'll give you a hint though; you should not have to do this for "State" universities and colleges. I have never seen a state-run college or university not having regional accreditation, unless it was just started. Regional accreditation takes two or more years to achieve. Here is a list of the six regional accreditation agencies and their website URL's:

1. Middle States Commission on Higher Education
(www.msche.org)
2. New England Association of Schools and Colleges
(www.neasc.org)
3. North Central Association of Colleges and Schools
(www.ncahlc.org)
4. Northwest Commission on Colleges and Universities
(www.nwccu.org)

5. Southern Association of Colleges and Schools (www.sacs.org)
6. Western Association of Schools and Colleges (www.acswasc.org)

You may see a pattern in their names as they cover different "regions" of the United States. Thus the term "regional" accreditation is appropriate.

National Accreditation

National accreditation is similar to regional accreditation but it has a national focus rather than a regional focus. National accreditation is a solid accreditation standard, but often does not carry the same level of acceptance as regional accreditation. In most cases, credits earned from a nationally accredited school may not be able to be transferred to a regionally accredited school. Most national accreditation agencies are recognized by CHEA. Again, you can get a list on the CHEA website (www.chea.org).

Keep in mind that the focus with national accreditation is a bit different. National accreditation usually focuses on specific types of education, such as career schools and colleges, continuing education and training, independent colleges and schools, occupational education, and distance education.

Specialized (Programmatic) Accreditation

Specialized accreditation is focused on a specific area of study, such as business, law, engineering, healthcare, education, and several others. Specialized accreditation is similar to national accreditation in that it has a national focus rather than a regional focus, but in a specific subject area.

One thing to note though, many schools that have regional or national accreditation may also obtain specialized accreditation for some of their programs. The reason is that specialized accreditation adds an additional level of acceptability for those programs. For example, a school with an engineering program can gain additional recognition by achieving accreditation through the Accreditation Board for Engineering and Technology (ABET). A school with a business program can gain additional recognition by achieving accreditation through the Accreditation Council for Business Schools and Programs (ACBSP). There are several others, to include faith-related and career-related accrediting organizations. I have seen graduate programs that require you to have an undergraduate degree from a school that is not only regionally accredited, but also has a specialized accreditation, such as in business and engineering programs.

Most specialized accreditation agencies are recognized by CHEA. To determine if an organization is recognized by CHEA, visit their website at www.chea.org.

Other Accreditation

In addition to regional, national, and specialized accreditation, there is another scope of accreditation. There are accreditation agencies that provide accreditation to schools that offer courses that meet national standards or offer Continuing Education Units (CEU). These are not college level programs. They usually fall under the area of professional development and continuing education. I will not go into detail on this since this book is focused on college level education. But I wanted you to be aware of these organizations. They provide a great service. Two such organizations are the International Association for Continuing Education and Training (IACET) and the American National Standards Institute (ANSI).

Caution about Accreditation

There are some "so-called" accreditation organizations that have a very similar name to some of the recognized accreditation agencies, but they are not recognized. In addition, there are other self-proclaimed accreditation agencies that appear to have an impressive or official sounding name. Degrees from schools that obtain their accreditation from these organizations are not worth the paper they are printed on. I would prefer a school to not have any accreditation at all rather than trying to persuade people that they have a valuable accreditation. As I previously mentioned, if you want to know if an accreditation agency is recognized or not, I strongly suggest visiting the website of the Council for Higher Education Accreditation (www.chea.org).

Other Acceptability Considerations

There are two additional important items about accreditation you need to be aware of when researching and selecting a school. First, if you are pursuing a degree in an area that usually requires you to get a professional license from a state organization, you should find out if the degree offered by a school you are considering is recognized in other states. For example, there several schools in one state where you can earn a law degree to practice law in that state, but those degrees are not recognized in other states. With those degrees you would only be able to practice law in that state where you earned the degree. Another example includes nursing schools. I have seen where some nursing programs in one state are not recognized in other states. This caution also applies to other fields that usually require a state-level professional license, such as real estate, accounting, and other medical fields. Second, there are some professional certifications that require a specific level of education. In addition, these professional certifications will only accept that education from schools that meet a specific set of criteria. One example is in the area of Medical Assistants. Not all schools that offer programs in this area are acceptable towards that professional certification.

The bottom line is that if you are pursuing a degree that may require a professional license or you may want to pursue professional certification in that area, it is extremely important to make sure the program you take is acceptable to other states or to certification programs. Do not just take the word of the school that their program is accepted. Do the research yourself. Check with other states executive departments that issue professional licenses. Check with the certification program administrative staff. If you get into a program that is not acceptable, you may be severely limiting your opportunities. The time to look into this is when researching the schools, not after you enroll or finish.

Degree Mills

Degree mills, also known as diploma mills, are schools that usually offer college degrees at a ridiculously low cost. They are not worth the paper they are printed on. I have seen some of these schools offer doctorate degrees for as little as $2,000. It is a waste of money. Those degrees are worthless! They may claim to have some type of accreditation, such as independent accreditation, but it is usually as worthless as their degree. Many of them claim to have legal authorization to confer degrees in a particular state. That simply means they have a business license, not accreditation. If you are approached by one of these schools, my suggestion is to run. You simply will be wasting your money. Always check their accreditation.

Chapter 7
About Online Education

Today, in the day of the Internet, you can complete your college education entirely from home over the Internet, from anywhere you are located. And when I say "entirely", I mean your complete education, from an associate degree through a doctorate degree. All you need is an Internet connection. This has been an interest of mine for a while. I have both taken and have taught courses on-line. It is a very interesting concept. Instead of sitting in class and listening to a professor lecturing, you are sitting at home and the interaction between you and your professor is over the Internet. There are so many opportunities available to you now that you didn't have in the past without having to relocate to another city or state. Most colleges and universities, to include public, private, for-profit, and even Ivy League offer degree programs on-line. It is amazing what is available to you these days. There are some degree programs that are not offered on-line, and you would not want them offered on-line. For example, medical doctor, nursing, veterinary medicine, and law are usually in-residence programs. You would not want a doctor operating on you that got their degree on-line. However, if you were planning on going into these areas, you may be able to reduce your education costs by taking some of your general education courses and electives on-line. You will need to check with your school to see if this is acceptable.

When taking courses on-line, there are two types of instruction, synchronous and asynchronous. Synchronous courses are courses that require both you and your instructor to be on-line at the same time and interacting. For example, you may be watching a live streaming video or audio lecture or a chat session and are able to ask questions in real time. Asynchronous courses do not require you and your instructor to be on-line at the same time and interacting. The instructor may record those video and audio lectors and you can watch them at just about any time of the day or night. You can still ask questions via e-mail or posting them on a discussion board, but you will have to wait for your instructor to log in and answer them, which is usually within a day. With synchronous courses, there are usually scheduled days and times that you have to log in and meet with your instructor and other classmates. Asynchronous courses offer the advantage of flexibility. You can log in at any time and do your assignments. There is usually a schedule for when assignments are due, but you do not have a set time when you have to be on-line. This is a huge advantage to those who have a job or a family. You can work full time and get your education at the same time. So when you are researching on-line schools, it is important to find out what type of instruction they provide. And if it is synchronous, find out what kind of scheduling is required to make sure it fits in your schedule.

Now let me debunk a myth. There is a myth that getting an on-line degree is not as good or accepted as getting your degree the traditional way. That is incorrect. When you get a degree on-line, the degree does not say it is an on-line degree, or does your transcript identify the courses you took were on-line courses. It is the exact same degree, carries the same weight, and has the same accreditation as if the degree was earned in class. Courses taken on-line are just as transferable as courses taken in class. The only thing that might hint to someone that the degree was earned on-line is if the school was based in California and you live in Florida, which should not make a difference. It is still an accredited degree.

There are some additional little-known benefits to on-line programs. In many cases you will have a much larger selection of programs and courses to choose from. In addition, you are not stuck to a single school. You have a lot to choose from. On-line courses often cost less than in class courses. Usually in-state and out-of-state tuition rates may apply. However, I have seen schools that apply their in-state tuition rate to on-line courses no matter where you live. Another benefit is that you will be able to connect to people all over the world. Your classmates may not only be in other states, but could be in other countries. This is a learning experience in itself.

Sometimes schools offer courses where a part of your course involves attending a class and part of the course is taught on-line. This is known as a blended or hybrid course. It gives you the best of both worlds. In most cases you don't spend as much time in class. I have personally attended and have taught these types of courses. It is a great experience but it does take away some of the flexibility of a fully on-line course.

I have one huge caveat about on-line programs – they are not for everyone. You have to have a lot of self-discipline and internal drive. You cannot be a procrastinator. I read somewhere that taking on-line courses will teach you self-discipline. That is something that cannot be taught. You either have it or you don't. Often it is something that you develop over time as you mature. If you have the drive to get your degree, you have one important aspect of what it takes for on-line courses. However, it still may not be enough.

Types of On-Line Learning Activities

In this section I will cover some of the types of learning activities you will experience in an on-line course. You will not find all of these activities in all on-line courses. It is up to the school and course developer as to what learning activities are utilized in a course. Keep in mind that these are only some of the more common types of activities you may see in an online course.

1. Reading Assignments. This should be fairly obvious. Your course may use a textbook or provide reading materials that can be downloaded, or it may include links to online materials to read.

2. Videos and Audio Lectures. You may be required to view on-line videos or listen to audio lecture recordings. These may be created by the school or your instructor, or they may be a resource on line.

3. Discussion Board Activities. A discussion board is sort of like an on-line bulletin board or social media board that students can post to. Normally, the instructor will post a topic or set of questions for the discussion board activity. Students will be required to create an original initial post on the subject. In

addition, students are usually required to post constructive feedback and remarks on one or more of the other student's initial post. The whole point of the exercise is to start a set of discussions between the students, much like you would have a discussion in a traditional classroom setting. You would be surprised as to what you can learn in these types of activities.

4. Video or Chat Discussion. This activity is where the instructor and all the students would log into an on-line system at the same time and have a video discussion or chat discussion. Sometimes this is used individually between a single student and the instructor to have a meeting on a subject.

5. On-Line Projects. These can range from tiny weekly mini-projects or exercises to large multiple week end of course projects. These projects depend on the subject of the course. For example, in a web development course you could be required to build a web site for the final project. In a project management course you could be required to create a schedule or work breakdown structure for a weekly project. In a marketing course you could be required to create a marketing plan for a new product or service. As you can see, the projects can be very detailed and involved.

6. Essays and Reports. Similar to a traditional classroom course you may be required to write essay papers and reports. These would be turned in on-line for grading.

7. Quizzes and Exams. Also similar to a traditional classroom course you could be required to take quizzes and exams on-line. Depending on the type of test, it could be automatically graded by the Learning Management System or manually graded by the instructor.

As you can see - these learning activities are somewhat similar to the activities that you may participate in a classroom situation. The only difference is that you would be doing them on-line over the Internet.

Two Specialized Teaching Approaches

There are two types of teaching approaches that I use in the courses that I develop and teach. I am bringing these up in this book because these approaches are very effective and welcomed by most students. Not all schools are using these approaches, or using them to their fullest, and you may want to keep an eye out for them when researching your schools.

The first approach is called competency-based education. This approach is where on-line projects are used in teaching the subject matter as well as assessing the competency of the students. Quizzes and exams would not be used to assess the students. In my opinion, this is one of the best ways to teach the subject and to determine if it was learned by the students. A test can only measure what a student remembers. It does not measure what a student can actually do. For example, if you are taking a course in computer programming, which would best determine if you can actually write a computer program - a test on computer programming or actually designing and developing a fully functional computer program? I think the answer to this question is obvious.

The second approach is called experiential learning. I am not going to get really technical here, but this approach combines research, creativity and doing, and reflection on what you have learned into the learning activities. Reflecting on what you have learned allows the subject to sink in deeper, especially if you can apply the learning activity to a real-world activity that you would encounter on the job after you finish school.

Chapter 8
Cost

In this chapter I will discuss the cost of college and provide some information that you need to know and consider when deciding to get a college education. I will provide some very interesting information on tuition and fees that may surprise you. If anything it will give you some valuable insight to the cost of college and information to think about. I will also give you some ideas on how to finance your education without going into debt.

Tuition

Tuition is the term used by schools that refers to the cost of the education provided. Most schools charge college tuition by the credit hour. For example, if the tuition rate is $300 per credit hour, then a 3 credit hour course will cost $900 in tuition, "plus" any other fees they charge. Some schools charge tuition by course or program. There is one school that I am aware of that charges tuition by the term, no matter how many courses you are taking. This is very cost effective if you take three or more courses each term.

It is extremely important to see the cost of the tuition of all the schools you are considering and compare them. I know of one state where the tuition for their community colleges is $49 per credit hour. That would be $147 for a 3-credit course. So why would you opt to go to a school that charges $900 a course for your first two years of college? It won't make a difference in the quality of your education, but will drastically increase the size of your student loan debt.

In-State Tuition versus Out-of-State Tuition

Most "public" schools have two tuition rates, one rate is for in-state residents and one rate is for out-of-state residents. The out-of-state tuition rate is usually much higher than in-state tuition. Moving to the state will not automatically qualify you for in-state tuition. You usually have to be a resident of the state for a particular period of time, usually a year or longer. The main reason why in-state tuition is less than out-of-state tuition is that public schools are governed by and sometimes subsidized by the state government. This is considered a benefit for the legal residents of their state.

I have seen articles on the Internet on how to get around this. Don't take this advice. Not only is it dishonest, but it is illegal. Remember a public school is a government organization and you will be signing documents attesting to your residency. If you make false statements, that is perjury. It is not worth the risk. You don't want to start out your life as a criminal.

With that said, there are ways to legally be eligible for in-state tuition rates even though you are not a resident of the state. For example, some schools charge in-state tuition for their on-line courses, even for out-of-state residents. Some states and universities have agreements with other states and universities to offer in-state tuition rates to students. In addition, there are organizations that have been set up to establish reciprocity agreement programs with universities of various states that allow you to pay in-state tuition rates. There are usually requirements involved to take advantage of these programs, such as the degree you want to pursue in another state is not available to you in your state. You should check into these programs as they will save you a lot of money. The school you are researching should have this information as well.

Special In-State Tuition Programs for Non-Residents

Some of the larger reciprocity agreement programs cover specific regions in the United States. Below is a list of these programs as of the writing of this book.

Section 1 - About College

1. The New England Board of Higher Education (www.NEBHE.org) has a program titled the New England Regional Student Program (RSP) Tuition Break. The participating "New England" states include Connecticut, Maine, Massachusetts, New Hampshire, Rhode Island, and Vermont.

2. The Southern Regional Education Board (www.SREB.org) has two programs, the Academic Common Market and the Regional Contract Program. The Regional Contract Program is specific to health professions. Participating states in the region include Alabama, Arkansas, Delaware, Florida, Georgia, Kentucky, Louisiana, Maryland, Mississippi, North Carolina, Oklahoma, South Carolina, Tennessee, Texas, Virginia, and West Virginia.

3. The Western Interstate Commission for Higher Education (www.WICHE.edu) has three programs: 1) Western Undergraduate Exchange (WUE), 2) Western Regional Graduate Program (WRGP), and 3) the Professional Student Exchange Program (PSEP). Participating states in the region include Alaska, Arizona, California, Colorado, Hawaii, Idaho, Montana, Nevada, New Mexico, North Dakota, Oregon, South Dakota, Utah, Washington, and Wyoming. In addition, some U.S. Pacific Territories and Freely Associated States participate in the program.

4. The Midwest Higher Education Compact (www.MHEC.org) has a program titled the Midwest Student Exchange. Participating states in the region include Illinois, Indiana, Kansas, Michigan, Minnesota, Missouri, Nebraska, North Dakota, and Wisconsin.

If you are considering a program in another state, I strongly suggest that you look into the associated program for your region. A national initiative is in development by the National Council for State Authorization Reciprocity Agreements (www.NC-SARA.org). They are working together with the programs above to establish a nationwide program. You may want to look into program availability with this organization.

Additional Fees

In addition to tuition costs, there are often additional fees that are added to the cost. These include admission fees, graduation fees, transfer fees, technology fees, registration fees, student activity fees, and many others. Some of these fees, such as the admission fee, are a one time fee. Some costs are assessed each term or by the number of credits you are enrolled in. Some of these fees can be fairly sizable. I have seen schools that when you add the fees to the tuition, you have doubled your cost. The bottom line is that you need to find out what fees are required in addition to the tuition costs and calculate this into your total cost when comparing schools. You may be surprised by the final cost. And don't forget the costs of your textbooks and other course materials.

Large State Universities

One thing to keep in mind is that not all state universities are the same, especially when it comes to cost. They vary all over the place. I have seen state universities in some states have extremely high tuition compared to other states. I have also seen state universities charge different rate than other state universities "in the same state". In my opinion that is ridiculous.

The size and popularity of a state university will have an impact on the cost as well. For example, if a large state university has a popular football team that has won some championships - they often have a higher tuition, even with other smaller state universities in the same state. So - you have to ask yourself - is popularity of the university important to you and worth the extra cost?

As Seen on TV

There are several schools, usually for-profit private schools that advertise on television. That does not make them good or bad. It usually means they are very expensive. As you know, television advertising is very expensive and that expense is usually passed to the students in high tuition rates, and because they are "for-profit". This is something to keep in mind when considering a college or university.

A Financial Comparison of Public and Private Institutions

It is important to note that the tuition and fees at private colleges and universities are usually higher than at public colleges and universities. That <u>does not</u> mean that you are getting a better education. The old saying "you get what you pay for" does not apply to education. Remember, these schools are not subsidized by a government and the "for-profit" schools are in business to make money. I'm not saying that there is anything wrong with that. It is just something you need to keep in mind.

Schools, no matter the type, vary in size, demographics, degree offerings, etc. These are things that you can easily check out for yourself. In my opinion, one of the biggest things that often really set them apart from each other is cost. I have done a

Section 1 - About College

lot of research on various schools and it is a real eye opener. Let me give you some examples.

The chart below (split into two parts) shows the differences in costs for two for-profit schools, one non-profit school, an Ivy League School, and three public schools. I explain the differences in the schools in the paragraphs below the chart. Please keep in mind that these are just different schools that I randomly selected to compare. But it shows you how different one can be from another.

Degree	For-Profit #1	For-Profit #2
Associate	$35,000	$25,500
Bachelors	$32,000	$37,100
Masters	$21,200	$27,980
TOTAL:	**$88,200**	**$90,580**
Doctorate	Not offered	$57,830
TOTAL:		**$148,410**

Table 8-1

Degree	Non-Profit	Ivy League	Public
Associate	$20,400	$63,000	$6,240
Bachelors	$20,400	$63,000	$12,712
Masters	$18,720	$49,200	$6,238
TOTAL:	**$59,520**	**$175,200**	**$25,190**
Doctorate	$33,000	$49,200	$15,390
TOTAL:	**$95,520**	**$224,400**	**$40,580**

Table 8-2

For-Profit College #1 (Table 8-1): This is a business college and is "not" regionally accredited, but had national accreditation. They offer both campus and on-line programs. Their tuition is astronomical. Now pay attention to this. This is important. **They do not post their tuition rates on their website!** I had to call them up to find out this information. This is a huge red flag. If a school is not willing to post their tuition rates on their website, or, if it is extremely difficult to find the tuition on their web site, my suggestion is to run. They usually have something to hide, which is probably astronomical tuition rates. I would never pay this kind of money for a college degree from a school, especially one that does not have regional accreditation.

For-Profit College #2 (Table 8-1): This for-profit university has regional accreditation. It is one of the largest on-line schools around. They also advertise on TV. You may have even seen one of their commercials on television many times. Yes, they are accredited; but the cost is still outrageous. Remember what I mentioned above in the section titled "As Seen on TV".

Non-Profit College (Table 8-2): Here is an example of a private university, which is a large on-line private Christian university that also advertises on television. Yes, they are accredited; and yes their tuition cost is better than the for-profit examples above. But the cost is still too high in my opinion. Just because they are a faith-based school does not mean their tuition is reasonable. However, I do believe this school is a very good school though.

Ivy League School (Table 8-2): This is a private university, which happens to be one of the Ivy League schools. The cost shown in the table is for a basic degree program that is non-professional. A professional degree would be much higher. Yes, they are accredited; and yes their tuition is ridiculous. And what blows me away is that they get a ton of money each year in endowments. I previously talked about endowments earlier on.

Public College/University (Table 8-2): Looking at the table above, I am sure you see a significant difference between a public college and the rest. Why would anyone pay $20,000 to $60,000 for a two-year associate degree when you can get one for a little over $6000 or less at a public college? It does not make sense. In one state I researched the tuition rates for their community colleges and it was $49 per semester hour. That's $2,940 for an accredited associate degree! I always suggest that you do your first two years at a community college and then transfer to a regular four-year college or university. It is much more cost effective, even if you are planning to go to an expensive private or Ivy League university. Also, I previously mentioned in Chapter 5 that some community colleges are converting to state colleges and offering four-year bachelor degree programs, which are even more cost effective. In the example in the table, the associate degree is from a community college and the bachelor's, masters, and doctorate degrees are from different state universities. See what happens if you shop around! There is no rule that says you have to get your different degrees all at the same school. And yes, they are all fully regionally accredited.

Financing Your Education

This section will be fairly short. I will not be telling you how to finance your education, but give you some ideas and things to think about. There are many books on this subject alone and I'm very disappointed in most of them. Many of them tell you of various ways to go about paying for your education. They cover scholarships, grants, work study programs, and student loans. The thing is – they don't provide you any additional or better information than what you can get through the financial aid office at a school. So save yourself some money and talk to the financial aid office at your school rather than buying one of those books.

When it comes to financing your education, my suggestion is to stay away from student loans as much as possible. You don't want to be paying for your education for 20 years or more after you graduate. Don't be caught in the trap from those admissions advisors that will tell you that you will get such a high paying job when you graduate that it will take no time to pay off your loans. Remember, they are sales persons and a lot of those schools rely on students getting student loans to pay their high tuition costs.

Apply for scholarships, grants, and work study programs. These don't need to be paid back. Get a part-time job to help pay for your school. If you are going to attend school on-line, get a full-time job. Plan your education carefully. Seek out those public schools where the cost is much lower than private and for-profit schools. Join the military. In addition to serving your country and giving something back, you will be able to earn education benefits to help pay off a college education and gain some great experience for your resume. Go to a community college for your first two years. It is usually the cheapest tuition around and there is no need to go to an expensive four year university for the first two years - especially if you are paying for it.

There are huge benefits to paying for your college by working your way through college versus getting trapped in student loans. Here are just a few:

1. The obvious one - no student loans. You will not have this burden after you graduate.
2. Gain experience for your resume. This will look good to employers after you graduate.
3. You will appreciate your education because you earned it and you paid for it yourself!

4. A job you are working during school could turn into a career. Many have!

5. You will be able to start building your professional network and even make some friends.

The bottom line is that you really can get your education and completely stay away from student loans if you want to.

Chapter 9
School and Course Quality

This is a subject that I can write an entire book on - and actually I am! But that book will be for schools and course developers to help them create high quality courses and programs. This chapter comes before the section on finding and selecting your school because these are some important things that you should keep in mind when evaluating schools. This is one subject that I spent a lot of time researching and have even experienced some of these issues myself as a student. The problem with some of these issues is that you will not be able to know if they are applicable to the schools you are researching until you start taking the courses. You might be able to find out some of the information from reviews by other students. But remember, you don't have to stay with program or school if you are dissatisfied with them. As I have previously mentioned, I have withdrawn from programs and schools within one or two weeks of starting their classes. A few of the schools I dropped were even state universities. So let's get started.

1. The courses in general are of poor quality. They are unorganized, do not provide very good instructions, don't spell out expectations well, and the course materials and information from the instructor contains numerous grammar and spelling

errors. I do not expect perfection because I am not perfect, but when I see a large number of these issues in a course I have to question the quality of the course. How can an instructor grade on grammar and spelling when the course contains numerous problems.

2. The courses required textbooks, but they were hardly used, extremely expensive, not current, and of poor quality. I have even recently seen a course that used a textbook that was almost 30 years old, and it was a computer programming course. There is no excuse for this with what is available today.

3. Some schools are moving from using textbooks to using what is called "open educational resources". These are open source and free. However, the quality of these resources was lacking, they were often not current, and the materials did not quite fit into the course well. In addition, the links to these resources sometime disappeared. The school's intent for using these resources is to reduce or eliminate the costs of textbooks for students, but the quality of the courses suffers greatly.

4. Earlier I mentioned my support for competency-based education and experiential learning. To me, this is extremely important in a course. I do not care for courses where all you do is read a book and write essay papers or read a book and just

take tests. In my opinion, these are poor courses and students are really missing out on a quality education. This is especially true for courses that should be hands-on, such as programming, education technology, project management, and other technical and business courses. I do not like courses where my entire grade depends on how well I did on tests. Remember, tests only measure what you can remember - not what you can actually do!

5. Degree programs sometimes lack flexibility and are structured in a way that don't make sense. For example, there are some bachelor's degree programs currently available that only require 33 to 36 hours of courses in their major subject - out of a 120 hour degree program! They allow more electives than they require for their major. In my opinion, these are very weak and poor degree programs. I have seen programs that required courses that did not quite fit into the degree program. These courses were a waste of time because they do not cover real-world skills or topics and do not benefit a student's career. I have seen some issues with graduate degree programs, such as the lack of flexibility in selecting courses. They will spell out exactly what you have to take. They don't offer any program electives. In addition, there are some graduate programs where some of the courses are "introductory" courses. In my opinion, all introductory courses should have been taken care of in the undergraduate programs. Graduate degrees are advanced degrees

and should not have any of these introductory courses. The bottom line when researching schools is to look at the structure of their programs and see if they have any of these issues.

6. High cost does not mean high quality. I mentioned this before - just because a school charges high tuition rates does not mean their programs and courses are of high quality.

7. I saved the best for last. In my opinion this is a huge problem with colleges and universities today. To save money, even though their tuition cost is going up, they are outsourcing their courses. Yes - they are hiring companies to teach their courses for them. These companies, called Online Program Management (OPM) companies build and teach courses for many colleges and universities throughout the country. You may not know this because they have the specific college's brand name on the course. Sometimes you can tell by looking at the URL where the course is being taught at. The kicker is that the instructors don't work for the colleges and universities - they work for the OPM companies - AND - the OPM companies are NOT accredited! Personally, I don't see how they are getting away with this. If you find out that a school is doing this, I would suggest seeking another school. It is possible that sooner or later the accrediting agencies will shut this down, making those degree programs worthless. If I am paying a college for an

education, I want the college to offer it and the instructors that work for the college to teach the courses - not some unknown unaccredited outside company. That's what I am paying the big tuition bill for and I would think you would want the same.

Chapter 10
Final Thoughts about College

In the first chapter of the book I mentioned the main benefit of having a college degree is that it will provide increased opportunities and earning potential in your career. One important related point is that the higher the degree you have, in most cases the more it increases the opportunities and earning potential you will have in your career. An individual with a master's degree will have more opportunities and earning potential than an individual with an associate degree, or a bachelor's degree. Now I'm not saying that you need to go out and get a doctorate degree, unless you want to teach or do research. As I previously stated, a bachelor's or master's degree will take you a long way and may meet all of your needs. You will just need to decide where and how far you want to go. And keep in mind that most people stop when they finish a bachelor's degree, which is great and will definitely have a positive impact in regards to career advancement. However, the master's degree may give you the edge over those with an associate or bachelor's degree in most cases. There are some situations where a master's degree makes you over-qualified for a position and some employers will not hire you because of that. They think that the first chance you have to get a better job; you will be out of there. I personally believe they are nuts. I am sure there have been some cases out there where this has happened, but I am also sure it is not the majority of the cases. I have hired a lot of people in my career and I would welcome someone with an advanced degree anytime - providing they can do the job. I would also say that if someone won't hire you because you have an advanced degree, then they are not worth working for. To me, that would be a huge red flag about an employer if they felt threatened about your degree. But, you have to decide for yourself as to what is best for you. You can always stop at the bachelor's degree level and get your graduate degree later. This gives you time to assess your situation. There are many job posting sites on the Internet. I would suggest that you go out and research educational requirements for some of the positions you may be interested in.

Additionally, having a college degree does not guarantee that you will be able to get work. As you look through those job postings, most, if not all of them will require experience. You may wonder how you would get that experience if you are just starting off as a college graduate. There are many ways, such as getting a part-time job while attending school, volunteer work in an area relevant to you degree subject, work study programs, and internships while in college. My son worked as a volunteer for six months while working on his AA degree. He later landed some part-time and project work. By the time he finished his bachelor's degree, he had over three years of work experience. Another place to get good experience is in the military. You can easily get your degree and several years of experience in the military. And a lot of organizations like to see military experience in resumes.

Section 2
Selecting a College and Degree Major

There are two major decisions that need to be made before you go to college. You need to pick a school and a degree major. The purpose of the chapters in this section is to provide you information that will help you make those decisions. There are no hard-fast rules or specific steps that you need to take to make these decisions. People make these decisions all the time and for a wide variety of reasons. The most important reason should be that the school and degree major you select meets "you're" specific needs.

Similar to the previous chapters in this book, you will not get hard rules on exactly how to pick a school or degree major, but you will get some needed information so you can ask the right questions and make a sound judgment on doing this yourself. You will have the information to be able to formulate the questions that need to be asked when talking to schools - and again, based on "you're" specific needs.

I want to start off by putting a thought into your head, especially for those of you who think you need to attend a "big name" university. As you read the remaining chapters in this book, keep in mind that if you have a degree from a big name university, it "may" help you get a job. There is no "guarantee" that it will. However, after you start working for someone it is your abilities and work ethics that keeps you there and moves you up the food chain in the company. The degree on the wall will have nothing to do with that. If you can't do the job or you don't have good work ethics, it will not matter what school you went to.

Before selecting a school, it is extremely important to research the school in detail. Don't just pick it because you heard it was a good school. Research the school. You should find out what they offer up front to make sure they offer a program that meets your needs. You need to find out if the school is accredited, and if so, what type of accreditation. You need to find out the cost of going to the school. Will you be able to afford going to the school, or will you have to take out a large student loan to attend? Does the school have a political bias? (They won't tell you this. You have to find this out yourself through research.) What is the history of the school? Have graduates been able to find work after they finished? There are numerous things you should find out about a school before selecting the school. And again, don't just take their word.

Research the instructors at the school. Do they have "real-world" experience, or have they spent their entire adult life going to school just to teach? Research the degree programs. Do they require a healthy amount of courses in your major field of study, or do they require courses that add no value to your degree?

This section will provide you the information you need to help prepare you to make a sound judgment on picking a school and your degree major.

Chapter 11
Picking Your Degree Major

In this chapter I will give you some things to think about when selecting the field of study that you may want to pursue in college. The first part of this chapter may turn you off a bit, but please keep reading and you will see where I am heading with this. So let's dig in. You probably have heard that "you should pursue an area that you are very interested in and passionate about". For the most part, I do not agree with this idea. I have a strong interest in fishing and photography, but due to the heavy competition and the limited number of jobs, it would be very difficult to pay the light bill or put food on the table in those professions. You have to be very, very good to be a paid professional fisherman or photographer. It is like being a rock star - you won't get the big gigs unless you are real good and people know you. Now I'm not saying that you should never pursue your interests in those fields. You just may need to wait for the right time and place. Let me tell you a few true "real-world" stories about this.

Some Real-World Stories

What I said about being interested in photography earlier is true. The first overseas military base I was stationed at in the

Air Force was in Okinawa, Japan. While I was there I took some photography classes in college and purchased some really nice photography equipment. I really enjoyed it and thought that I was actually fairly good. When I returned to the United States I decided to try my hand in the photography business on a part time basis so I obtained a freelance photographer business license and did some work on the side. To make a long story short, it only lasted about a year, and I didn't make much. I did have a few odd photo jobs, such as taking personal portraits, and even got some work in the area of glamour photography taking some portfolio photographs of some models. But the competition was brutal and the number of available jobs was minimal. If I had tried to do it full time, I would have probably been one of those "starving artists" you've heard about. It's still an interest of mine and I occasionally dabble in it once in a while, but that is not what is putting food on the table and paying the bills. One good point here is that if you want to test the waters, you should "try" something new like this on a part-time basis and don't quit your full-time job.

Here is another "real-world" story. Several years ago I knew a person that moved from Arizona to Washington State, where I was living at the time. This person had a degree in Anthropology. In Arizona she worked with the government on many Indian reservations and burial grounds. I'm sure it was

Chapter 11 - Picking Your Degree Major

very interesting work and a passion of hers. When she moved to Washington, it was very difficult for her to find work in her expertise. There is not much call for anthropologists in the state of Washington. Pretty much the only jobs available in that state are museum curators, which are all probably already taken, and college professors; but she didn't have a high enough degree to teach college. My point is that she had a good degree that she was very interested in and passionate about, but had very limited options and "locations" for work. The degree was not that marketable in a different state.

And here is one more real life story. A while back I was in a barber shop getting a haircut. The barber was young and struck up a conversation with me and we ended up talking about education. He said that he was currently working on his AA degree at a local community college and when he was done he would transfer to a four-year college to pursue a degree in "music literature". He wanted to write music. It was something he was very interested in and also passionate about, but I think you see where I am going with this. How many people really make it big in the music industry? That is something you have to be extremely good at and well known because it is a very competitive area. Remember the term I previously used, "starving artists"? Well there is a reason for that. And again, I am not saying that he or anyone else should never pursue their passion.

I can tell even more "real life" stories, but I think you get the idea here. These and many other areas have limited "opportunity" and "marketability". Now don't get me wrong here and throw the book in the fireplace. I want to say again that you should never pursue areas that you are interested in or have a passion for. But think about this - you do need a roof over your head, food on the table, and have to pay the light bill, especially if you have a family. In other words, you need to be able to live. What I am saying is to make yourself marketable <u>first</u>, then pursue your passion. Doing this even makes pursuing your passion easier because you will have a roof over your head and food on the table. And you never know, you may find something that you really like doing while pursuing a marketable education. That happened to me. If you read the preface to this book, you will see that in the pursuit of my education I discovered a field that really interested me (computers) and the rest is history. It took me a long way in my life, even before I retired from the Air Force. After retiring from the military, I have had a successful career in the information technology field, to include owning and operating a systems development and consulting company that's been in business for over 25 years as of the writing of this book. So I am just throwing out the idea of temporarily postponing the pursuit of your passion field for a little while. Get your degree; get a career; then go for it.

I want to give you one more real life example when it comes to having a marketable degree. If you read the "About the Author" section at the end of the book, you may recall that I have a BS degree in Management Information Systems, a Master's Degree in Engineering Management, an Education Specialist Degree in Information Science and Learning Systems, several complimentary certifications, and good experience. During the economic environment of the great recession (mid to late 2000's), which resulted in high unemployment and high inflation, I had no problems finding work and have even turned down some great opportunities. I do not attribute that to my good looks. I attribute that to my very "marketable" credentials. I am sure that if my credentials were not marketable, I would have had a lot more difficulties and my life would have been quite a bit different.

Government Study

The US Department of Education released a report that is very relevant to this book. One part of the report is very relevant to this chapter in regards to selecting a degree major, and another part is relevant to another chapter in regards to

Section 2 - Selecting a College and Degree Major

selecting a college. The findings of the report are based on a survey conducted in 2012 of more than 17,000 college graduates who graduated in 2008. With that number of respondents, the statistics should be quite accurate.

In this chapter I make the point that selecting a degree that is marketable will provide increased opportunities and earning potential. The findings of this study support that statement. The study compares graduates with a major in a STEM subject (Science, Technology, Engineering, and Mathematics) to graduates with a non-STEM major. The results are interesting but not surprising to me.

Their Finding on Annual Salary: The report shows that graduates with STEM degrees had an average annual salary of $65,000 where non-STEM degree graduates were $49,500. Of the STEM degrees, graduates with degrees in computer technology and engineering ranged from $72,600 to $73,700. Of the non-STEM degrees business and healthcare fields ranged from $55.500 to $58,900, and degrees in education and humanities ranged from $40,500 to $43,100. This definitely shows that your choice of degree major has an effect on your earning potential.

Their Finding on Employment: The report also shows that graduates with STEM degrees were employed more and spent less time out of the labor force. Graduates with STEM degrees were unemployed for about 4.6% of the time and out of the labor force for about 8%, where graduates with non-STEM degrees were unemployed for about 6% of the time and out of the labor force for about 10.6%. In addition, the report showed that graduates with non-STEM degrees reported working more multiple jobs than graduates that had STEM degrees.

The bottom line of this report is that the selection of your college major does have an impact on job opportunities and earning potential. The report is titled "Baccalaureate and Beyond: A First Look at the Employment Experiences and Lives of College Graduates, 4 Years On", dated July 2014. It was released by the US Department of Education, National Center for Education Statistics, Institute of Education Sciences.

As of the writing of this book, the report is available at http://nces.ed.gov/pubs2014/2014141.pdf.

Just in case the government moves the report, I posted a copy on my professional website at
http://www.GaryHarris.com/perm/IES_Study.pdf.

Section 2 - Selecting a College and Degree Major

Four Ideas

When it comes to selecting a field of study, I have four ideas that you may consider.

1. Select a field of study that is marketable. Selecting a marketable field of study will help provide the benefits I outlined in chapter one, increased opportunities and increased earning potential. As I previously mentioned, once you have yourself established, then pursue your passion. Many college degree programs include open elective courses, which allow you to take courses in any subject you want to take. You can earn a minor in a subject that is not related to your major. However, I would not suggest this. I would take elective courses or earn a minor that enhances the marketability of your degree. For example, a degree with a major in business administration with a minor in accounting would be more marketable than a degree with a major in business administration and minor in music history. Make sense?

Don't pick an area just because it sounds cool. Many people earn degrees in subjects and later discover that they really don't want to do that type of work. For example, engineering sounds real cool, is a great career to get into, and is very marketable. However, you may not have the aptitude for engineering and it may not be what you want to do later on. I personally know people with great engineering degrees that are not working as engineers, even though they can.

I have one additional bit of caution when selecting your major - be careful to not over-specialize. What I mean by over-specializing is selecting an area that is limited to a specific subset of a larger area. For example, Accounting and Marketing are subsets of Business Administration. Network Administration and Database Development are subsets of Information Technology. Specializing would make you more valuable in positions specific to those subset fields and would provide increased earning potential in those subset fields. However, in some areas you may be reducing one of the main benefits mentioned in chapter one – reducing the number of job opportunities available to you. For example, if you are interested in accounting, which is a good and marketable field, and decide to pursue a degree in accounting, you may be limiting your opportunities to only accounting positions. It would be very challenging if later in your career you wanted to do something different outside accounting. In this case, you could get a degree in Business Administration with a "minor" in Accounting. This gives you your accounting credential and also increases your job opportunities beyond accounting. Another example would be a degree in database systems, which would limit your opportunities to only database related positions. In this case you could go for a degree in Information Technology with a minor in database systems. This would give you the database credential and also increase your job opportunities beyond working with databases only. Get the idea?

However, there are some fields that you would want to specialize in. For example, engineering would be an area where you would want to, and usually have to specialize in, such as mechanical, electrical, or civil engineering. Some areas of law, medicine, and psychology would benefit by having specializations as well. You will need to do some research to select the best direction.

2. Don't be afraid to change your major. If you start a degree program in one subject area, and after taking a couple of courses you determine that you really don't see yourself doing that type of work later on, don't be afraid to change your major. Make sure you put a lot of thought into your decision and don't overdo it. Changing your major too many times can have a huge impact on when you complete your degree. It may add months or longer to your degree program and graduation date. So don't overdo it.

Chapter 11 - Picking Your Degree Major

Many people start college not knowing what they really want to study. That is ok. If you are in that boat, don't worry. There is nothing wrong with this. There is no rule that says you must know your major when starting college. That is a good reason to start off by pursuing an associate degree in a general subject such as general business, information technology, psychology, or education. In working on a general subject, you may discover an area of business that would interest you and you may want to pursue a minor in, or find out that the general area is not for you.

If you cannot even narrow it down to a general area, you can pursue an Associate of Arts (AA) degree. This is basically a liberal arts degree where you would knock out all of your general education courses and is usually easily transferable to most four-year programs. You could then use your open electives to try out courses in various areas to see which area you might be interested in. An AA degree will allow you to transfer to a four-year program in virtually any field, but you may need to take some additional lower division courses that you didn't take in your associate degree program. Remember, all degrees require some amount of general education courses. An AA degree will most often cover them all. Don't be afraid to try new areas. If you think it may interest you, you can give it a try.

There is a tool out there called an "Interest Test". This is a test that many schools offer that try to help you determine an area that you may be interested in. These tests ask a wide variety of general questions. There are no "right" or "wrong" answers. They compare your answers to individuals who have taken the same test and that are in a variety of different industries. If your answers mostly match the answers of others in a certain field, then it "may" indicate an area that you might be interested in. If you take one of these tests, don't take the results as gospel. These are not 100% reliable. They just give you something to consider.

One of the best ways to help you decide is to get on the Internet and do a lot of research about different areas. Talk to people in those areas. Set up visits to companies to see what they do. You may be shocked to see that what you read about a person does in one profession compared to what they really do in real life. Sometimes it is vastly different than you think. Doing some volunteer work, internships, and part-time jobs while pursuing an associate degree are also good ways to research different areas. The military is another option you can take. You can spend four years in the military racking up some great experience while researching areas you may want to study.

3. Don't be afraid to make other changes. Don't think that once you start a program or school, you are stuck with them.

You are in control here. I have personally dropped programs and changed schools that I was not satisfied with. I was accepted into three different Ph.D. programs and ended up dropping out of those programs within the first or second course. In those cases I was extremely dissatisfied with the program and instructors. I expected a lot more, especially when I was paying $1,500 to $2,500 for a single course. But my point is that you are in control. If you are in a program or a school that you are not getting what you expect out of it, you can drop it. Remember, they work for you. You are the one paying for their service of providing you an education. If they cannot provide that service to your satisfaction, you can fire them. But be careful that you are not just jumping around from one school to another. It will have a toll on your education and can extend your graduation date similar to changing you major. It is important to thoroughly research schools before committing to a program. In the next chapter I will provide some very detailed information and ideas that will help when selecting your school.

4. Spend a lot of time researching and thinking. I cannot stress this too much. Today we have the Internet. There is so much information available to you. You can research just about anything on the Internet. I always suggest going out to job posting sites to research education requirements for different types of industries. These job sites have a lot more information than just education requirements. They tell you specific skill sets that they are looking for, other experience, specific knowledge in tools and technologies, and much more. One thing that many people don't catch is that it will give you an idea of the "number" of potential opportunities available in specific fields and in specific geographical locations. For example, if you enter "computer programmer" in a job site search engine, one of the things it comes back with is the number of positions found. You can usually further narrow your search by geographic location and get a count in your area. You can do this for several fields to get an idea of the opportunities available to you. I also suggest going to more than one job site since they often have different listings. But keep in mind that the count you get is for a specific snapshot in time. The count could be different tomorrow, next week, or next month. But it will give you some ideas as what is available.

You can also make contact with individuals in fields you are interested in on professional social networks, such as LinkedIn. I would suggest staying away from the non-professional social networks that do not have a career, business, or professional focus. The people on the professional social network sites have a wealth of information in their career. Many of them are willing to answer questions about their career. Make sure you ask about growth opportunities in their field.

Chapter 11 - Picking Your Degree Major

Another good source is the US Department of Labor, Bureau of Labor Statistics. They have a ton of information about careers on their site BLS.gov. They even have industry growth statistics as well. The only thing to keep in mind is that some of their data lags behind a couple of years at times. But it is a good research source.

The other thing you should do is spend a lot of time thinking about your research and about yourself. If you have narrowed down your selection to a few different areas, think about each one separately. Ask if you can see yourself doing this type of work for a long time. This is really important. I know a few people that have college degrees in some really good areas that have a lot of opportunities, but they have no desire to work in those fields. They worked in those fields early on in their careers, but decided later they do not want to work in those fields. So it is important that you do a lot of soul-searching when making your decision. Do you see yourself doing that type of work in ten or twenty years? Do you see yourself doing that type of work when you are 40 or 50 years old? What is the outlook of the profession ten to thirty years down the road? These are just some of the questions that need to be answered. And don't forget the other idea I brought up - it is ok to start college without knowing exactly what you want to do. You can get in and start taking general education courses. Some schools require you to declare a major. In that case, simply go for the AA degree. You can always change your major with the school. But get in and start. Don't wait!

Final Thoughts

When you started reading this chapter I hope you didn't expect me to tell you what major you should pursue. That is a decision only you can make. A "how to" book or my book cannot make that decision for you. One size does not fit all and every person and situation is different. What I have tried to do is give you information to think about so you can make a sound judgment yourself. I am sure that after reading this book you will be well armed with the knowledge to do your research and make that decision.

Chapter 12
Selecting Your School and Getting In

Getting into college can sometimes be a little tricky. Schools often have specific requirements that must be met before you can be accepted. The higher the school considers themselves in status, such as an Ivey League University, the harder and stricter the requirements to get in. This is a pet peeve subject of mine. I personally believe that if you meet the minimum requirements set by the state and accreditation board, you should be able to get in. Period! Let's get into this a little deeper.

College Admissions

All colleges and universities have admission requirements and they vary from one school to another, and some can be extremely challenging. It is very important that you know these requirements up front prior to starting the admissions process. Let's talk about some of the potential requirements.

All schools require an admissions application of some sort, which usually requires the payment of an admission fee. These days, most admission applications are online so you can complete them from home. In addition to the application, you may be required to submit other documents, such as entrance

Section 2 - Selecting a College and Degree Major

exam test scores, college transcripts, letters of recommendations, a statement of intent or objectives, and other possible items. I have covered transfer credits and the importance of having a good GPA in an earlier chapter of the book and will be covering entrance exams later in this chapter. It is important to know these requirements in detail when selecting a school.

You may have noticed two items I mentioned, letters of recommendations and statement of intent or objectives. These are usually required when applying to a graduate degree program. These requirements vary greatly from one school to another. In regards to letters of recommendations, you may be required to submit from two to four or five, depending on the school. The school will usually dictate as to who they need to be from, how many to submit, and their format. A statement of intent or objectives is a one to two-page essay that you put together to describe your objectives and goals as it relates to the degree program you are applying for. I have two suggestions here. First, read carefully the requirements for the essay several times prior to writing it. Schools usually provide a detailed list of items that needs to be addressed in the essay. It is important that you address each and every one of them. Second, after you write it, go over it many times. Read and revise it as necessary to get it right. Make absolutely sure that there are no exaggerations or misinformation, and no spelling or grammar errors. These are

Chapter 12 - Selecting Your School and Getting In

sure fire ways to get rejected from the program. Also, get several people that are good at writing to review and proofread it. Do not submit this essay until it is absolutely perfect because it can mean the difference from being accepted or rejected.

There is one more thing you need to be aware of about admission requirements. Sometimes it may be possible to get a waiver for an admission requirement. Some schools even spell them out in their brochures or catalogs. For example, I have seen schools that will waive the requirement for an entrance exam if you have a high enough GPA from your previous degree or high school. (This is another reason to maintain a good GPA.) Keep in mind that just because a school does not state that a requirement can be waived, does not mean they won't consider granting a waiver. It never hurts to ask. Let me give you a couple of examples. My son was interested in a master's degree program that required a specific GPA to be accepted. He did not have that GPA, but he was close and he had a good reason why he did not have that GPA, which was a medical situation in his last year of school. The school admissions documentation did not mention anything about waivers. I suggested that he apply for one and he did. He was accepted into the program. Here is another example. If you complete a master's or specialist degree and plan on applying to a doctorate program, especially at the same school, one requirement may be to submit and have a specific score on the Graduate Record Examination (GRE) entrance exam. If so, you my want to request a waiver for the GRE test. The purpose of a GRE test is to determine if you have the abilities to handle and be successful in graduate school. If you earn a graduate degree, especially at the same school you will be seeking a doctorate degree, what other proof is needed that you can handle graduate school. So I would suggest applying for a waiver. Again, it does not hurt to ask. I am sure that you can take and pass the test, but I don't see a point in spending the time and money on it if it is not needed. The important thing about requesting a waiver is that you must have a solid and sound reason for requesting it. If you feel you do have a good reason for a waiver, go for it. It may save you some time and money, and get you in the program that you want to be in.

Research the Schools

As I previously mentioned, before selecting a school, research it in detail. You will want to find out everything you can about the school before attending. If you don't, it could be very costly in the long run and a big waste of time. You will want to make sure that you get the quality education that you pay for and deserve. I will give you some items to think about when researching your school. Some of these items may not be applicable if you are just taking online courses and not going to be attending classes at the school.

First, look into the history of the school. Check to see how long they have been around and how long they have been accredited. Check to see if they ever lost their accreditation, and if so, for what reason. Check to see if they have had any other problems in the past, such as lawsuits or criminal activities. Don't just go by the information listed on their web site. Do some research on the Internet; check with the local Chamber of Commerce; contact the Better Business Bureau; check with the state and federal department's of education. Some schools may require more research than others. In my opinion, public institutions usually require less research.

Look into where the school spends their money. You may get an idea of this by their tuition cost. If their tuition is fairly high compared to other schools and they even solicit and receive donations and endowments, where is their money going? It is obvious they are not reducing tuition. Do they have a large and fancy football stadium or sports complex with coaches making a million dollars? Do they have several 5-star cafeterias on campus? Do they have several large new buildings on campus? Do they bring in big name speakers that charge $300,000 for a 1-hour speech? You get the picture. Find out where they spend their money in relation to the education they offer and the tuition they charge. You might find out that it may not be worth it.

Later I will be discussing researching the instructors at the school you are considering. You should also look at the makeup of the instructors at a school. Accredited schools require a certain percentage of their instructors to have doctorate degrees. Is the school you are considering have a high number of instructors with doctorate degrees or not? Do they have a high number of adjunct (part time) instructors, versus permanent instructors? What is the percentage of instructors to administrative staff? In other words, are they spending more money on administration versus academics? This could mean that the class sizes are larger than at other schools. These are some things you should think about.

You should consider the location of the school and its surrounding area. Remember you may be there for two to four years. You will have to decide if you will be comfortable with the location of the school. For example, I personally do not like big cities. I would not attend a school that is in a large city. Some people may not have a problem with the size of a city, or may even prefer it. You have to decide for yourself what will work for you.

Chapter 12 - Selecting Your School and Getting In

Check out the facilities on campus. Are they kept up or are they deteriorating? Is the grass cut? Is there any graffiti on the walls? This may be another flag for you. If you are going to stay in the dormitory, and if you can, try to visit some dorm rooms. This is going to be where you will be living for a while. My son stayed at a dorm for one term that was a disaster. The elevator was broken and run down and his roommates were pigs. Needless to say, the following term he got a place off campus.

Another item to consider is the activities available to you on campus. Since you are going to be there for a while, you may want to get involved in some clubs or sports activities. This will provide you with a break from your school work. You may even be able to join a group or club that is related to your degree major. This will allow you to learn even more by sharing ideas and even give you a start with your professional networking.

Most schools offer some form of job placement assistance for their graduates. In some cases it may just be in the form of career counseling and resume assistance. Some schools either have a pseudo-job placement office or work with one or more job placement agencies. The level and type of job placement assistance varies from one school to another. In researching potential schools, you should inquire into the type of assistance they offer and how successful it has been for their graduates - especially if you are going to be paying a lot of money to go there.

Research the Programs

When selecting a school, you should look at the structure of the degree programs they offer. As I previously stated, no two colleges are the same. The same goes for the degree programs they offer. Look at the required courses for the degree major. If you are interested in getting a degree in computer science, you would want a substantial amount of the required courses to fall in that area. If one school requires 30 credits to be in the area of the major and another school requires 50 credits to be in the major, I would seriously consider the school requiring the higher amount. It is a stronger program.

Another aspect you should look for are required courses that have nothing to do with your major, or don't even add any substantial academic value to your degree. For example, if you decided to pursue a degree in engineering, and the school requires courses in gender studies or social justice, run from that school. This tells me that they are not serious about your education.

Chapter 12 - Selecting Your School and Getting In

The important thing is that when you earn a degree in a specific subject, you should walk away with a solid knowledge of your area of study. The more courses you take in your major, the greater the knowledge you will attain from the program. You should not waste your time on useless programs or courses that will not prepare you for the real-world.

You should also look at the courses themselves. How are the courses structured and taught? Are the courses mostly made up of reading assignment and tests? Or do they have quite a bit of hands-on work? A test only measures what you remember. Project work measures what you can actually do. You can evaluate this by asking the school for copies of some of the courses in your major subject to evaluate. If the school is not willing to share this with you, then that tells me they may have something to hide.

Research the Instructors

Often you will not have a chance to select your instructors. However, when you are conducting your research on schools, many schools will list the biographies of instructors that teach in specific programs. I would suggest reviewing them. This is something I wish I had done before applying to one of the Ph.D. programs I was accepted to. Let me explain. The first

Section 2 - Selecting a College and Degree Major

course I selected after being accepted into the program was a course in Database Systems. I figured this was going to be an easy "A" for me since I have been designing and developing database systems for over 20 years. When I was in his lectures, I was totally lost. I could not figure out what the instructor was talking about. And when I would ask for assistance, I was told not to worry about it. Needless to say, I was getting very frustrated and should have dropped the course, especially since the course cost me over $2,500 out of my pocket. I didn't do too well on the final exam and actually thought I failed the course, but the instructor gave me a "B-" for my final grade, which surprised me. That is not considered a good grade at that school at the Ph.D. level. I later went out and read the instructor's biography. Yes, he had a Ph.D., but he had no practical "real-world" experience. His entire adult life was spent as either a college student or college instructor. I didn't see anywhere where he designed and developed a database system for a real company. From that point on, I decided that I will look for instructors that have actual hands-on, real-world work experience. It has been my experience that they are much better instructors because they have done the things they are teaching.

There are websites online where you can find out about instructors at certain schools where students rate their professors. You can also find out information at some social networking sites as well. You just have to be careful reading these and don't take them as gospel. Often students that don't do well and receive bad grades will usually give the professor a bad score, and vice versa. So - if there just a handful of posts like that, I would ignore those posts. Chances are they are just a few students that didn't do well in the course and took it out on the professor. However, if there are 200 bad posts for one instructor and they all basically say the same thing, then you might want to take that into consideration.

Aggressive Admissions Tactics

I want to talk a little bit about admissions tactics because that is often another noticeable difference between public and private institutions. When you contact a public institution and speak with an admissions advisor, there is a very noticeable difference than when you speak to an admissions advisor at a private school, especially a for-profit school. An admissions advisor at a public school really acts like an admissions advisor. You can tell they are trying to help you out in making your decision without any pressure.

In my experience, when you talk to an admissions advisor at a for-profit school, you are basically talking to a sales person. They use high-pressure strong-arm sales tactics to try to get you enrolled quickly. Before you even get started asking your questions they are trying to get a lot of personal contact information about you, such as your address and phone number. And you know that if you give them your contact information you will get regular sales calls from them later if you don't enroll that day. I would not give them any information up front. In addition, they also often start talking to you early about getting student loans to finance your education. Keep in mind, these are sales people and are usually working off scripts and have an answer for just about anything. I have personally seen this. In some cases they are not very knowledgeable about their programs at all. If the information is not on their script, they change the subject or tell you that if you give them your number they will find out and get back to you. I even spoke with someone at a school that didn't even know who they were accredited by, but they insisted they were accredited.

Do your research before contacting a school, particularly with for-profit schools. Here are some suggestions:

1. Before you dial their number, block your phone number (usually *67) so they cannot get your phone number from their caller ID. They do this. It has happened to me. They will ask for your contact information. Do not give them your contact information. Otherwise, you will get a lot of phone calls

from them in the future with high pressure sales tactics. If they insist on getting your information, or they won't talk with you unless you give them your information, hang up. That is a red flag and you should not have to give up your contact information just to get information about the school. They will try to trick you into giving them your number by saying something like they need your number to call you back just in case you get disconnected from them. I tell them that I will call them back in that case.

2. Ask a lot of questions. If you cannot get answers, run!

3. Stay in control of the conversation. If they get control of the conversation, it will be a lot harder to get the information you need.

4. Most important thing to remember: DO NOT let an admissions advisor convince you that you will not have any problem paying off student loans after you get their degree. That is hogwash! Many people fall into this trap and end up losing in the end. As I have said before, getting a degree does not guarantee employment, or good employment.

Another admissions tactic that many for-profit schools use to get your contact information is through "lead aggregators", especially on the Internet. When you use search engines to research schools on-line and you click on a link that you believe is for a specific school, often you will be taken to page that may appear to belong to a school, but it is not. The page will often have a short form to fill out so you can receive information about the school. Or, you may click on a link and may get a list of schools and when you click on a school link, it takes you to a similar form to fill out. In many cases these are not websites belonging to the schools. They belong to lead aggregators, and there are many of them out there. Try searching the term "lead aggregator" on the Internet and you will see what I mean.

A lead aggregator is simply a marketing firm that collects contact information on potential students and re-sells them to the schools. In some cases, they may sell the names and contact information to multiple schools. I have some personal experience with lead aggregators. If you take the bait and fill out that online form, you may receive numerous calls, sometimes from numerous schools (accredited and non-accredited), about various programs. In many cases, these calls come from those high-pressured admissions advisors I previously talked about. I would suggest not filling out any forms on the Internet to get information about the school. Go to the school's website yourself. It will save you a lot of frustrating calls.

Entrance Exams

I am not going to spend a lot of time on entrance examinations, but wanted to provide you with some basic information regarding them. Entrance examinations are used by many colleges to select students for admission into a college or specific program. These exams are usually not the only deciding factor for admission and are often combined with other factors, such as your GPA, in making an admission decision. It is important to note that <u>not</u> all schools and all programs require entrance exams. Many schools and programs do not require them. As part of your research you will need to find this out, and if required, take the necessary tests. There are plenty of courses, books, and study materials available to you to help you prepare for the exams that you will need to take. A school that you are interested in will be able to provide you with the information on entrance exams they require. In addition, there is a lot of information about entrance exams on the Internet as well.

There are basically three categories of admissions tests, undergraduate, graduate, and professional. At the undergraduate level, there are two widely used entrance exams. They are the Scholastic Assessment Test (SAT) and the American College Testing (ACT) tests. The two widely used entrance exams for graduate programs are the Graduate Record Examination (GRE) and the Graduate Management Admission Test (GMAT); the latter normally is used for business and management programs. For professional degree programs, the entrance exams include the Law School Admission Test (LSAT), the Medical College Admission Test (MCAT), the Dental Admission Test (DAT), the Optometry Admission Test (OAT), and others. As previously mentioned, you will need to find out which test, if any, is required for entrance into the program you are interested in pursuing.

I personally do not believe in entrance exams. In my opinion, I think they are worthless and they are a way for schools to weed out students they don't want. In my opinion, they don't work. There is no way a test can tell if you will do well in school or will even finish school. I completed three undergraduate degrees and never took the ACT or SAT to get into the schools. To date, I have completed two graduate degrees with a high GPA and currently working on a PhD and have never submitted a graduate entrance exam. So that should tell you something about entrance exams.

Personally, I don't believe I would do very well on an entrance exam. Unlike an entrance exam, in a course you study the materials in detail before taking quizzes and exams. You know what will be on the exam. There are courses and materials

Chapter 12 - Selecting Your School and Getting In

that you can get to help you with entrance exams. However, they don't cover "exactly" what will be on the exams. They can only cover what types of information can be on them. The organizations that administer the entrance exams keep the information on them very secure. You don't know what will be on the test until you have it in front of you. Keep in mind that there are many schools out there that don't require entrance exams. Also, I have noticed recently in the news that some schools are dropping their use. I applaud those schools.

Red Flags

Below is a list of red flags on important items to consider when searching for a school or degree program. Some of these items may not be important to you or some of them may not be applicable to you or the school and program you are seeking. For example, if you will be attending online, then the on-campus activities would not be important to you. This is a good list to go through and use when researching your schools and programs.

- It is extremely hard to find information on a school's website.
- The school's website lacks certain information requiring you to call them.

Section 2 - Selecting a College and Degree Major

- The credit transfer program is extremely restrictive.
- A school does not offer the degree or program you want.
- The school has a history of political bias.
- The school is not regionally accredited.
- If needed, the school does not have the specialized accreditation you need.
- The tuition is extremely expensive compared to other schools.
- There are a large amount of additional fees in addition to the tuition.
- The tuition and fees are not easy to find and understand on the website.
- The school is outsourcing their courses to Online Program Management (OPM) companies.
- The school has extremely challenging entrance requirements.
- The school has a high reliance on entrance exams.
- Past problems in the school's history.
- Instructor's credentials / distribution not adequate.
- Instructors have limited, or lack real-world experience.
- School spending too much money on non-academic items.
- School facilities in poor condition.
- Lack of or limited activities on campus.
- Lack of or limited job placement assistance.

- Major subject areas do not make up a substantial amount of a degree program.
- Required courses are not relevant to the degree program.
- The degree programs are not very flexible.
- The school will not provide sample copies of course syllabi.
- The courses are solely based on reading and tests or reading and essay papers and have very little hands-on activities.
- Admissions advisors have high-pressure admission tactics.
- The school uses Lead Aggregators.

Final Thoughts

One important point that I want to make - if you don't live near a public institution, don't think you are stuck going to a private or for-profit school. As I previously mentioned, most public colleges and universities offer complete programs on-line. For example, my son lived at home and finished his bachelor's degree in information technology at a state university 500 miles away. Later he completed a master's degree at a state university in another state. As of the writing of this book, I am working on my PhD at a university located in another state.

Section 2 - Selecting a College and Degree Major

Make sure that you visit websites that belong to the schools you are researching. Most college and university websites will tell you everything you need to know. They should provide complete information about the school, to include accreditation, which should be one of the first things you check out. Their websites should cover the programs they offer in detail, to include admissions requirements. They should provide tuition and financial aid information, to include how to apply for it. If you go to a website that does not include this information, especially tuition, be very careful. To me that is a red flag. If they do not post their tuition on-line, or if it is very difficult to find, there is usually a reason for that. It probably means that their tuition is extremely high. They don't want to chase you away before they have had a chance to try to convince you on the phone to apply to their school along with large student loans.

Section 3
In College and Beyond

Assuming that you have selected a college and a degree plan and you have applied to and have been accepted into a degree program, now it is time to do some planning. Planning your education is just as important as researching the schools and degree programs. Planning your education will help ensure that you make the best decisions on the courses you take and when to take them. It will help make your college experience enjoyable and productive. And - it will help raise the quality and value of your degree.

In this short section I will provide some simple methods on planning your education that includes creating a plan, and selecting and sequencing your courses. If you just pick your courses at random from the course catalog, you may end up having to take more courses than you need which could delay your graduation and add cost to your education. You could also miss out on course opportunities that could add value to your degree. I will also provide some information regarding things you may want to consider doing after you graduate other than just seeking out work. There are some things you can do after you graduate which can add value to your college degree and will make you more marketable and expand your potential opportunities and advancement. After college - you should not stop learning.

Chapter 13
Planning Your Degree

Ok, you have selected your route (area of study) and your school, now it is time to plan your trip. Let me start off by saying that you don't have to plan your entire college education for each and every term. But you do need to do some planning. Planning your education will provide structure to degree program and take a lot of guesswork out of selecting your courses. It will help you make good decisions.

Degree Plan

It is very helpful if you create a degree plan before you start. A degree plan is simply a list of courses you will need to complete to earn your degree. Some schools have blank forms for you to fill out to create a degree plan. You can even find them online. Some schools will provide sample degree plans that you can use or modify to meet your needs. Or you can just use a blank piece of paper.

Important Note: As you select courses for your degree plan, make sure that you pay close attention to the prerequisites for the course. A prerequisite is a course, prior experience, or level of knowledge that is required before taking a specific course. For example, an introductory course in accounting is usually required before taking any other accounting course. The introduction to accounting would be the prerequisite course. You will need to take the prerequisite courses first before taking more advanced courses. In some cases, if you have prior experience in an area, the school may accept that as a prerequisite. For example, if you worked part time creating web pages for a company, they may accept that experience before accepting you in higher level web development courses. It does not hurt to ask if you feel that you have prior relevant knowledge or experience. It could save you some time and money taking the prerequisite course. But make sure you do have that knowledge. If you just tell them you have that experience or knowledge so you don't have to take the prerequisite course, and you don't have it, it could make taking the advanced courses much more difficult, which could possibly hurt your grades. As an instructor, I have seen this happen many times. It can simply be avoided by taking the prerequisite courses. Keep in mind that they usually do apply to your degree program and they usually don't add to the number of courses you need to graduate.

Selecting your courses is a very important task. In many cases you will be required to take specific courses and have no choice in the selection, such as with core courses and general education courses. In some cases you may have a choice of some core courses and general education courses. You should carefully review and research the options and select the best courses that will meet your long-term career goals. In other words, select courses that will benefit you after you graduate.

Don't just select the easy ones for a good grade. Those may help your GPA, but may not benefit you after school. Some employers do look at the courses you took in college and that information may be used in making a hiring selection. There will be courses that are in both the "easy" and "difficult" categories that you will be required to take. Keep these in mind when selecting your courses each term. You may want to equal out your course load with a combination of "easy" and "difficult" courses, otherwise it may be overwhelming for you and it may have an impact on your degree program or GPA.

Here is a very simple way to create your degree plan:

1. List all of the General Education courses that are required for the degree. In some cases it will simply say something like "6 semester hours from natural sciences". This gives you the option to select the classes that you are interested in. For example, if you like geology you can take geology instead of chemistry or biology for your natural sciences.

However, it is important to check with your Academic Advisor to make sure the courses you select meet the requirements.

2. List all of the required core courses for your degree. In some cases, you will be given a selection such as: "Choose course A or course B"; "Choose three courses from the following list"; "Choose 15 credits from this category". In these cases, read the course descriptions and prerequisites carefully. Try to determine which courses will meet your career goals the best. For example, if pursuing a degree in Information Technology and interested in website development, and you are provided the option to take a web programming course or a desktop programming course, you should select the web programming course because it is directly related to your goal of becoming a web developer.

3. List all program electives for your degree. Remember, these are electives that you select that fall under the major area of your degree program. I would suggest selecting courses that will benefit your degree program and meet your needs. For example, as in #2 above if you are interested in web development, you could take all of your program electives in web development courses.

Chapter 13 – Planning Your Degree

4. For open electives, I would simply set up a "placeholder" for those courses and not list the specific courses themselves. Remember, an open elective can be any course you select. It can be in French Literature or even underwater basket weaving. These do not have to be selected now, but I would show in your degree plan that there are courses you need to take there. As I previously mentioned, I would suggest taking courses that enhance your degree. French Literature may be fun and interesting, but it will not help you be a better web developer or mechanical engineer. When it comes time to take an open elective, you can select it at that time based on your needs, interests, and course availability.

5. For all courses listed in your degree plan, list the prerequisite courses required for each course. After you list the prerequisite courses, make sure that you have selected and listed them in your degree plan. Remember, you will need to take them first before taking the more advanced courses in that area.

6. Now that you have all the courses listed, you can then sequence them. I will cover this a little later.

The next thing to do in your degree plan is to sequence the courses. This is where you list them in a specific order. This would be the order in which you take the courses.

Sequencing Your Courses

The next thing to think about is the order in which you take your courses. This is very important. I strongly suggest that you take your required courses (core courses and general education courses) first and save your electives for last. Remember, core courses and general education courses are those courses that you "must" take to get your degree. If you use up all of your elective courses in the beginning of your program and just have core and general education courses remaining, then you may run into scheduling problems that may lengthen the time for when you graduate due to course availability. By saving your electives for later gives you a lot of flexibility. For example, if you have taken all your elective courses and are down to a few core courses, and they are not being offered in the term you are registering for, you may have to wait an additional term or longer before they are offered, impacting when you will be able to graduate. If you have taken all of your required courses and only have electives left, you can take any course you want and not have an impact on when you graduate.

An important aspect of the order of your courses is the prerequisites. As previously mentioned, a prerequisite is one or more foundation or lower-level courses that must be taken "before" a more advanced course can be taken. For example,

Chapter 13 – Planning Your Degree

before you take English 200, you may be required to take English 100 and 101 first. Many courses in the second year of college and beyond have prerequisites. Look at the core courses and general education courses first. Identify all the prerequisites for the advanced courses and sequence them to be taken first. This will reduce the chances for any delays in your degree completion. A good plan in what order to take courses is 1) general education courses; 2) prerequisite courses; 3) core courses; 4) program electives second; and 5) open electives last. This does not mean you should not take any electives early on. You may need to slip in an elective once in a while due to availability of core and general education courses. But don't use them all up early on.

Important Note: Keep in mind that not every course is offered every school term. Because of this you may need to modify your sequence a bit as you start taking courses. Some schools publish a course rotation schedule which tells you what courses are offered during specific course terms. You should ask and try to get a copy of this if it is not published on their website. You can also check the schedule of past terms to see when courses were offered. Keep in mind that this all subject to change. The school can change a schedule. A course can be cancelled because not enough students enrolled in it. But if you created a solid flexible degree plan, you will be ready for any changes. You will be able to easily select a replacement course and modify your sequence with little impact to your degree program.

Now that you know how to sequence your courses, go to your degree plan and sequence the courses you selected. Once you have sequenced your courses, you are almost done with your degree plan. You should then show your degree plan and discuss it with your Academic Advisor. Your Academic Advisor will have some insight into the scheduling of courses and may suggest some valuable tweaks to your plan.

Once you have sequenced your courses and discussed it with your Academic Advisor, you are done with your degree plan! When completed, you can use your degree plan like a roadmap to get you to the end of your path to your degree. In addition, like a roadmap, you can change your path or direction. You can change courses if they are not required, such as electives. Your degree plan is a living document. Just be very careful when making changes. It can have an impact on when you complete your degree and it could add cost to your overall program. For example, if you took course A and course B in preparation to take course C because they are the prerequisites for that course, and later decide to change course C to course D, it is possible that courses A and B are no longer needed and some new prerequisites may be required. So be careful! The less you change your plan the better off you will be.

Course Load

Now that you have your degree plan completed, it's time to start taking courses. Each term you will select courses from your degree plan to take. You should follow the sequencing as close as possible unless a course is not offered in a term that you would like to take it in. Then a tweak to your degree plan may be needed. But - there is one thing you need to take into consideration when registering for courses each term - your course load.

Course load refers to the amount of courses you take in a single term or semester. As part of your planning you will need to take this into consideration. There are two important points here: 1) You do not have to take the same amount of courses each term; and 2) The courses that you should take, the courses you want to take, and the courses you have to take don't always coincide. Also in most cases, there are not a minimum number of courses that you need to take. The reason why I say "in most cases" is that schools normally do not dictate a minimum course load. A minimum course load is often dictated by the type of financial aid you receive. For example, if you are receiving a grant, scholarship, and even a student loan, you will need to take a minimum course load to receive the financial aid. You should check with your financial aid office to find out if this affects you.

Another thing you need to consider is how fast you want to complete your degree program. The more courses you take each term - the quicker you will finish your degree. A typical bachelor's degree program is 120 semester hours, which usually consists of 40 courses at three semester hours each. The usual structure is to take 10 courses a year for 4 years. This is why it is known as a four-year degree. This is called a full-time load. You can do this by taking five courses each term and take the summer term off. Or you can take four courses a term and two courses during the summer term. Or five courses one term, four in another term, and one during the summer. There are a variety of combinations. Schools that are on a quarter semester hour structure have their ways as well. Now if you take two courses a term, then it will take you longer than four years to finish your degree. Working adults taking courses often fall into this category. If you are not working and considered a full time student, five courses per term should easily be achievable. You may even be able to squeeze in a course or two during the summer terms, which would allow you to complete your degree earlier. If you are working, then two to three courses each term may be a better fit for you. The bottom line is that you have to create a course load that fits into your life and career goals. It is important that you do not overload yourself with more courses than you can handle. It will have an impact on your health as well as your GPA. So don't overdo it. Your health and GPA are very important.

There are two other things you should take into consideration when selecting your courses each term. These include the complexity of the courses and the amount of course work involved. Let's take these items one at a time. When I speak of complexity, I am referring to how hard or how easy a course is. This is something that is different to each person. You will have to do some research and decide for yourself if a course is hard, medium, or easy based on your knowledge and background. The suggestion is to select a combination of easy and hard courses each term. For example, if you decide to take four courses in a term, I strongly suggest that all four courses would not be considered hard subjects. A mixture of each would be best, such as two hard courses and two easy courses. A hint - don't use up all your easy courses at the beginning of your program similar to not using up all of your open electives. The second item I mentioned is the amount of coursework involved in a course - and this is different from complexity. Some courses have a lot more work than other courses. For example, a writing course may require you to write a research paper each week and a management course may only require one term paper at the end of the course. You should be able to see the difference in the courses I'm referring to here. The amount of coursework is not something that you would get from the course description. You will have to do some research to find out. There are two ways you may be able to find this information. First, you can ask other students who have already taken the course. Second, you can check with the instructor and see if you can get an advance copy of the course syllabus prior to enrolling in the course. I have found that instructors are often willing to provide one. Oftentimes instructors post previous versions of the syllabus on the school's web site. Once you have this information, you can select your courses. Similar to selecting the courses based on complexity, you should do the same with selecting courses based on the amount of coursework. You want to select an even amount of courses here - about half of the courses that require a lot of coursework, and about half that have a lower amount of coursework. Sometimes these courses fall in line with the selection based on complexity. The bottom line is that you should take these things into consideration when making your course selections each term.

In many cases, the courses that are being offered in a specific term will determine your course load. Colleges don't offer every course each and every term. They schedule the courses from term to term. Often a course may only be offered during one term each year. Courses that you want to take or need to take may not be offered in a specific term. You will have to plan for these things by sequencing your courses correctly during your planning, which I discussed earlier.

Chapter 14
In College

This chapter will provide some tips and ideas to help you to be successful in your courses. I can write a whole book on this subject, and may do so. The subjects in this chapter cover aspects of college that I have seen as a college instructor that students have often struggled with. If you can get a handle on these methods early on, you can be much more successful in your courses and even enjoy them more. I speak from experience not only as a college professor, but as a student.

Tips for Writing Projects and Papers

I am starting this section with an analogy. In the field of information technology computer programs are designed and developed by computer programmers. When a programmer writes a program, they just don't sit down and start coding. They are given a document called a "system requirements document". This document is a very detailed document that specifies what the computer program is supposed to do. It tells them the different modules and functions of the program; it tells them how to calculate specific formulas; it tells them what needs to be on the reports created by the program and how they are formatted; it tells them in every detail exactly what the program needs to do and how to do it. The computer programmer follows the requirements document to the letter in creating and writing the program. They do not subtract from the requirements and they don't add items to the program that is not in the requirements document. If they do, the programmers can get into a lot of trouble. I have seen programmers fired over not following requirements documents. With that said, when you are a given a project or writing assignment in a course, you should treat the assignment instructions document just like a programmer would treat a system requirements document. You should follow the requirements to the letter. If you do, you should do well on your projects and papers.

As an instructor for several colleges and universities I have seen and graded a huge number of projects and papers over the years. And what really surprises me is the high percentages of papers that are turned in that don't even meet the minimum requirements. When you are given an assignment for a project or a paper, the requirements are spelled out. The assignment requirements tell you exactly what is required. You should follow them to the letter when creating your project or paper. When you are done with your project or paper, you should be able to go down the list of the requirements, compare them to your final project or paper, and determine if you have covered all of the required items. You can use the assignment requirements like a checklist when you are done. If the instructor gives you a grading rubric, you should also review it in detail before you start your project or paper to see what the instructor will be grading you on. You should also use the rubric along with the assignment requirements to go over your project or paper after it is written and before you turn it in. By doing this you will be able to make sure that you have covered everything in the assignment and ensure a good grade. If there is "anything" in the assignment requirements that you don't understand, you should ask the instructor about it. Don't be afraid to ask questions. If you don't understand a requirement, how can you expect to get a good grade on your submission?

I had mentioned earlier that a computer programmer should not "add items to a program that the requirements document does not include". This is true for projects and papers in courses for several reasons. I get a lot of projects and papers from students that think that if they add more to their project or paper that is beyond what is required they will get a better grade. This is completely false. In many cases it is just the opposite. Many instructors will take points off for this automatically, especially if you are in a computer programming course. Another issue with doing this is that it adds time to your project. You may already be running close to the due date and you should not risk adding more time that may cause you to be late.

Now here is the big reason why you should not do this. Anything you add to your project or paper makes it subject to grading. If you add something to your paper that is not required and you get points taken off for it, it will reduce the final grade you receive for the paper - even if the rest of your paper is perfect. This means that if you would not have added the extra work "that was not required" you would have had a perfect paper. In addition, by adding items to your project or paper that is not required does not give you extra points. For example, if you had points taken off for a required item, but your added work was good, it does not add any points to the final grade. The bottom line is that you should not add more to your project or paper beyond what is required. It will not help you, but it could hurt you.

Plagiarism

As you may know plagiarism is basically copying somebody else's work. This includes copying from a book or someplace on the Internet. This could cost you anywhere from receiving a bad grade to expulsion from your school. You are usually allowed to quote somebody's work by enclosing it in quotes and providing a reference or citation to the work. But you cannot do this for your entire paper. In addition, you are usually allowed to paraphrase someone else's work. This is where you restate somebody else's work in your own words, but you are still required to provide a reference or citation to the work. Again, you cannot do this for your entire paper. I have received papers where the entire submission was just a rewording of a paper or multiple papers from the Internet. You cannot just change a few words and make it your own, even if you reference it. All of these methods are wrong and can easily be spotted and found by your instructors. Instructors even have tools that can easily spot this. Additionally, it's cheating and you are not learning anything. You are just learning how to copy someone else's work. It's just not worth it. If you need to research topics to write projects or papers, the best way is to read, study, and synthesize the various articles and books on the subject, then think about what you learned and how to apply it to the problem in your assignment, and then write from your own knowledge. You still have to reference your source. By doing this, you are learning the subject matter and are able to apply what you learned to resolve a problem. And just as importantly - you are not cheating and risking your college education or your reputation. And believe me - you will not be able to copy someone else's work when you get a job after you graduate. It's a good way to get fired or sued.

Internet Research and Computer Literacy

Two important skills that will greatly help you in college, and after college, are Internet research skills and computer literacy. Internet research is not simply typing something into a search engine and seeing what come back. It involves a lot more. In regards to using Internet search engines, you should lean how to really use them to filter the results and drill down to the results you really want. Go to the help page and learn the tricks on how to do efficient searches. For example, putting a plus sign in front of a word ensures that word is in the search. Putting a minus sign in front of a word removes that word from any searches. Placing a few words within quotes forces the search to look for those words in that specific order. There are several things you can do to narrow your search down to obtain specific results. Getting back a million search results does not mean it was a good search. Now you have to go through all those results to find what you are really looking for.

When reviewing and looking through your search results read each one very carefully before you click on the link to go to the web page. It may not be relevant to your research. It may simply contain a word you searched on. In addition, it could be a dangerous website that could infect your computer with a virus or worst. Don't click on any links that sound suspicious.

Chapter 14 - In College

Additionally, make sure that the source you use in your papers and projects are reputable and relevant to your work. It probably would not be a good idea to quote the Bubba's Beef Burger Bar website for a paper on building construction project management.

In reference to computer literacy, this is much more than knowing how to turn your computer on and cruising the Internet. It is essential that you have a solid foundation on various aspects of using your computer. This will make your job easier in college and beyond. Here is a short list of items that will go a long way in you life. You may be familiar with some of these items, but I have known students that don't know much about these items.

- Know the file system on your computer. Know how to create directories. Know how to save files on your hard drive and how to find them.
- Know how to do simple maintenance of your computer, such as defragging the hard drive, scanning the system and USB drives for viruses, and backing up your files to an external drive.
- Know how to take screenshots on your computer of the entire screen or individual windows. Know how to use a simple graphics tool to crop those screenshots.

- Know how to use the basic functions of a word processor, spreadsheet program, and presentation program.
- Know how to work on your computer without being connected to the Internet.
- Know basic Internet safety. Don't just rely on your antivirus Internet security program.
- Know how to install and uninstall programs on your computer.

Netiquette, Email, and Respect

There are tons of articles on the Internet about netiquette. I strongly suggest going out and reading a few of them. But the bottom line of netiquette is "respect". It is important and honorable to be respectful and civil to others, whether in person, in email, or on the Internet. I am not going to go into detail as to what respect, decency, civility, courtesy, or decorum is. This is something that you should have learned at an early age. If you follow these rules, it will take you a long way. There is no reason whatsoever to not follow these rules when you are talking to people, sending emails, or making posts in discussion boards. Just because something may be "legal" to do, does not make it right. Enough said.

Additional Suggestions

Here are some additional suggestions that will greatly help you be successful in college and beyond:

1. Take your college education very serious. It is one of the most important things you will do early in life that will have a huge impact on the rest of your life.

2. Don't be afraid to ask questions. If you don't know something, ask somebody. Don't guess.

3. A very important skill in college and after college is writing and public speaking. If you can do both well, you will go a long way in college and in your career. I've been teaching a long time and the one thing I see students struggle with is writing. In many cases it impacts their course grade in a substantial way. It is important to learn how to write well and to learn how to write well early on. The sad thing is a lot of what I have seen could easily be corrected just by simply using the spelling and grammar checker in their word processor. It surprises me how many students don't do this. But even with these built-in word processor tools it is important to learn how to write well without having to rely on these tools. This is one skill

that I strongly suggest getting good at as it will take you a long way.

4. Don't procrastinate! I see this so much as an instructor. I can often tell when a student has waited until the last moment to do their work and turn it in because their work shows this. I also get requests for extensions at the last moment with a variety of excuses. Most of these are not approved. So the bottom line is, don't wait until the last day to do your work. In my studies, my target is to have my work turned in at least a day before it is due, or earlier. That way, if something does come up, I have the time to deal with it.

5. As I mentioned earlier in the book, watch out for withdrawals and incompletes. These could have a negative impact on your education and career. In addition, monitor your GPA. If it looks like it is going down, work harder. Your GPA is important to your future in many ways.

6. If you are taking courses on campus, here are a couple of tips:

a. Learn your campus. Get to know your campus very well. Know where the major facilities are, bathrooms, eating establishments, library, and very importantly, the security office.

b. Get involved with school activities. This will help you keep focused on your studies and get you out of your room. One caveat though - do not over-do them to a point to where they are affecting your studies. Your studies are more important than extracurricular activities. If you belong to an organized church, many schools have groups of various denominations for meetings and bible study. Many schools have a type of student body activity office where you can get information regarding all the activities on campus, and sometimes activities off campus in the local area.

c. Don't do anything stupid. Be very careful with some activities, such as traveling on spring break or getting involved in something questionable.

d. If you feel that you are being treated unfairly or wrongfully by an instructor, talk with someone in the administration office. You are there to learn and don't have to take any abuses of any kind. Remember, they work for you. Your tuition pays their wages. But don't forget to be respectful.

e. This is probably the most important suggestion about taking classes on campus – keep in touch with your family and friends. This is very important because they are a great support system for you.

7. This suggestion may sound odd, but it is important - watch the news or read the newspaper regularly. You should keep abreast of what is going on in the world. I'm not saying that you should spend hours every day on this, but 30 minutes to an hour every day or two will be good. This will also enhance your education. You will be able to communicate better and be a better citizen. One caveat though - do not just watch one news channel or one political view of the news. That is what is causing a lot of problems in the world today - because people only have one side of the story. You need to have a well-rounded view of things going on.

8. My final suggestion is to have fun. Don't go to college and just study. Have some fun. Do something once in a while to get your mind off school. Go to a movie, or go bowling, go to a theme park, or visit with family or friends. It is important for your mental wellbeing and your studies to take a break once in a while. But like everything else, don't over-do it.

Chapter 15
After College

This chapter is devoted to making one simple point. And that point is, after college - don't stop learning! Continuing your education after college will benefit you in many ways. It is important for your career and your personal health to keep learning. You will be able to keep your skills sharp in your career. You will be able to keep up with new developments in your career. In some careers, such as Information Technology, continuing education is a huge "must" because technology is rapidly changing. You can also pick up new skills that will enhance your career. It will help you from becoming stagnated or stuck in a position. It will show your boss that you want to grow in your career. I am not suggesting that you go for another degree, which would not hurt, but there are other directions you can take to enhance your career.

Continuing Education

There are several opportunities for you to continue your education after college. Below is a list of the most popular opportunities.

Professional Development Courses

Professional Development Courses are usually focused on career development for advancement. They help with picking up new skill sets and knowledge to help move you forward in your career. In addition, they help you keep current in your industry. They are often taught by instructors either in a traditional classroom setting or on-line. Professional Development Courses are greatly beneficial to a career.

Continuing Education Courses

Continuing Education Courses are similar to Professional Development Courses, but have a wider focus. In addition to providing courses that cover career related materials, they also include soft skill subjects such using computers, business writing, or public speaking. Many of these types of courses are provided in an independent study format not taught by an instructor. Like Professional Development Courses, Continuing Education Courses are beneficial to a career.

Professional Certifications

Professional Certifications are special designations earned by individuals by meeting specific requirements, such as passing a certification test. They designate that an individual is qualified to perform a specific job role, such as accountant, can perform a specific type of task, such as project management, can work with a specific type of equipment, such as forklift operator, or can work with a specific type of product, often software, such as a database product. There are numerous areas and career fields that a person can earn a certification in. Many of them follow and enhance a college degree. Some job positions even require a specific certification before you can apply for the job. One important point is that a Professional Certification is not a license to practice in that profession. It is simply a designation signifying a level of expertise, skills, and knowledge.

Professional Associations

A Professional Association is an organization or society that is organized to support and foster a profession, occupation, or industry. There are literally hundreds of professional associations available to join. They usually require a nominal annual membership fee. With the membership you often receive many benefits, such as books, periodicals, job listing boards, and special interest groups that you can be a part of to benefit your career. Professional associations often offer Professional Development Courses, Continuing Education Courses, and Professional Certifications in the related profession. Professional

Associations are a good source to network with other professionals in your field. They often have local chapters that have regular meetings that you can attend and meet others in your profession. Professional Associations are a great source of continuing your education after you earn your degree. You can also join them while you are in school as a good resource for school projects. They often offer a student membership rate, which is usually far less than the regular membership rate.

Books and Periodicals

Another good source of enhancing your career after college is to read books and periodicals in your profession. This is a good way to keep up with new developments and to keep your skills and knowledge sharp. However, I would also recommend considering the earlier resources I mentioned.

Consider Another Degree

You might want to consider getting another degree. If you have an associate degree, I would suggest pursuing a bachelor's degree and not a second associate degree. If you have a bachelor's degree, I would suggest considering a master's degree. If you have a master's degree and do not plan on teaching or going into research, consider getting a second master's degree in a field that will compliment your first degree. This will often greatly enhance your career. For example, if you have a master's degree in information technology, you could get a second master's degree in business, computer security, or project management. Any of these degrees would go well in complimenting a master's degree in information technology. Or, if you are in the education field, consider getting an Education Specialist Degree.

The Bottom Line

The bottom line is to never stop learning. Not only will it benefit your career, but it will have a positive impact on your life in many ways.

Chapter 16
Conclusion

I told you this book would not be long, but it does pack a wealth of information. I hope it will be helpful to you in seeking your college degree. Remember, having a college degree will provide you with increased opportunities and increased earning potential in your career. Feel free to drop me a note and let me know what you think about the book at my professional website, www.GaryHarris.com. I also have links to universities, colleges, and community colleges on my website that you can use for your research. If the college industry changes a lot, I may update this book at a later date. Good luck to your in your endeavors!

About the Author

Gary Harris has over forty years of "real-world" experience in highly demanding positions in systems analysis and development, project, resource, and personnel management, management analysis, consulting, and education. Mr. Harris started his career in the United States Air Force as a munitions specialist at the age of 17. In that specialty, he worked his way up to managing several workshops and becoming the section chief managing two shops and controlling all munitions operations on the military base. Mr. Harris cross trained into the Manpower Management career field, achieving the position of Superintendent of Manpower on an Air Force Base managing over 5,000 manpower requirements assigned to 26 organizations. In that position he also headed several business/process re-engineering projects, cost comparison studies, and the implementation of total quality management programs in several organizations. Mr. Harris retired from the Air Force as a Master Sergeant.

After retiring from the Air Force, he spent three years as an employee of the State of Washington working in various Information Technology positions. In 1997, he started working full time in his own business, which he started in 1990 as a part time business before retiring from the military. For the next seven years he worked as a contractor, consulting and developing several high-end enterprise systems. Most of his clients were state government organizations for the State of Washington, to include the Department of Transportation, Department of Veterans Affairs, and the Attorney General's Office. Some of those systems he built then are still in operation as of the writing of this book. He also started designing, developing, and marketing his company's own line of commercial business software. Some of the software products even had a global reach with clients in seven different countries.

In 2007, Mr. Harris was contracted by a large nationwide on-line university to develop all of the on-line professional development courses for their new Information Technology Program. He personally developed ten courses and managed several subject matter experts to develop 25 other courses. He also was the instructor for the courses he developed. He later accepted the position of Dean of Business and Information Technology. He was in the position for two years up to the point they reorganized and moved the functions to Wisconsin. (The university is not mentioned to prevent any misconceptions or misinterpretations with the subject matter in this book.) Mr. Harris later worked with a professional association developing and managing the development and delivery of several courses and certificate programs. As of the writing of this book, he is teaching on-line courses for two state universities.

Mr. Harris earned his Education Specialist Degree in Information Science and Learning Technologies with a focus on Learning Systems Design and Development and an Online Educator Graduate Certificate from the University of Missouri earning a 4.0 GPA. Previously, he earned a Master of Engineering Management Degree from Saint Martin's University with a 3.63 GPA, a Bachelor of Science degree in Management Information Systems with a minor in Psychology from the University of Tampa with a 3.147 GPA, and an Associate of Applied Science Degree in Work Center Management from the Community College of the Air Force. He is currently pursuing his PhD in Information Technology with a concentration in Information Security Systems and to date has maintained a 4.0 GPA. He completed professional certificates in Advanced Project Management and Advanced Computer Security from Stanford University. In addition, he holds several professional certifications, to include Certified Secure Software Lifecycle Professional (CSSLP), Project Management Professional (PMP), Distance Education Certified Trainer (DECT), Certified Enterprise Integrator (CEI), and Certified Management Engineer (CME).

www.ingramcontent.com/pod-product-compliance
Lightning Source LLC
Chambersburg PA
CBHW020413080526
44584CB00014B/1311